From Autism and Mutism to an Enlivened Self

From Autism and Mutism to an Enlivened Self explores the importance of intimacy, interaction with the environment and the mind–body connection in early childhood development, with specific reference to autism. Built around a detailed case study of a severely autistic child, the book offers an illuminating account of the development and successful treatment of autism both from the perspective of the clinician and from the family.

In Part I, Diana Thielst (writing under a pseudonym) gives a description of her experience with her daughter who was autistic at birth, minimally verbal at age five, and did not respond to her name. She details the severe family stress and her ineffectual attempts to get professional help. Finally, she hears of consultants who may be able to help in St. Petersburg, Russia. Guided by the consultants, Thielst and her daughter then embark on a uniquely innovative method for Anna to both build a vocabulary and for the first time learn the value of coordinated and cooperative effort. Armed with a vocabulary and a long history of solo pursuits of organizing inanimate objects, Anna suddenly begins to explore "human" interaction as revealed in comics – a turning on to an emotional life of relatedness and intimacy.

In Part II, Joseph D. Lichtenberg uses his knowledge of neonate and early infancy to offer the reader an understanding of autism – its history – and a unique comparison of the normal well adapted neonate and infant at one year with the disrupted development of the child with autism. Lichtenberg's theoretical construct of three major pathways to a healthy adapted development breaks new theoretical ground and gives enrichment to a contemporary portrayal of the autistic experience.

With unusually rich clinical material grounded in accessible theory, the authors jointly offer a new perspective on understanding, treating and living with autism. *From Autism and Mutism to an Enlivened Self* will appeal to psychoanalysts, psychoanalytic psychotherapists and clinicians working with autistic children.

Joseph D. Lichtenberg, M.D., is Editor-in-Chief of *Psychoanalytic Inquiry*, Director Emeritus of the Institute of Contemporary Psychotherapy and Psychoanalysis, past President of the International Council for Psychoanalytic Self Psychology, and a member of the Program Committee of the American Psychoanalytic Association.

Diana Thielst, M.D., is a pseudonym under which the co-author of this book is writing about the treatment of her autistic daughter. She is a scientist and musician.

PSYCHOANALYTIC INQUIRY BOOK SERIES

JOSEPH D. LICHTENBERG
Series Editor

Like its counterpart, *Psychoanalytic Inquiry: A Topical Journal for Mental Health Professionals*, the Psychoanalytic Inquiry Book Series presents a diversity of subjects within a diversity of approaches to those subjects. Under the editorship of Joseph Lichtenberg, in collaboration with Melvin Bornstein and the editorial board of *Psychoanalytic Inquiry*, the volumes in this series strike a balance between research, theory, and clinical application. We are honored to have published the works of various innovators in psychoanalysis, including Frank Lachmann, James Fosshage, Robert Stolorow, Donna Orange, Louis Sander, Léon Wurmser, James Grotstein, Joseph Jones, Doris Brothers, Fredric Busch, and Joseph Lichtenberg, among others.

The series includes books and monographs on mainline psychoanalytic topics, such as sexuality, narcissism, trauma, homosexuality, jealousy, envy, and varied aspects of analytic process and technique. In our efforts to broaden the field of analytic interest, the series has incorporated and embraced innovative discoveries in infant research, self psychology, inter-subjectivity, motivational systems, affects as process, responses to cancer, borderline states, contextualism, postmodernism, attachment research and theory, medication, and mentalization. As further investigations in psychoanalysis come to fruition, we seek to present them in readable, easily comprehensible writing.

After more than 25 years, the core vision of this series remains the investigation, analysis and discussion of developments on the cutting edge of the psychoanalytic field, inspired by a boundless spirit of inquiry. A full list of all the titles available in the *Psychoanalytic Inquiry* Book Series is available at www.routledge.com/Psychoanalytic-Inquiry-Book-Series/book-series/LEAPIBS.

From Autism and Mutism to an Enlivened Self

A Case Narrative with Reflections on Early Development

Joseph D. Lichtenberg and
Diana Thielst

Routledge
Taylor & Francis Group

LONDON AND NEW YORK

First published 2019
by Routledge
2 Park Square, Milton Park, Abingdon, Oxon OX14 4RN

and by Routledge
711 Third Avenue, New York, NY 10017

Routledge is an imprint of the Taylor & Francis Group, an informa business

British Library Cataloguing-in-Publication Data
A catalogue record for this book is available from the British Library

Library of Congress Cataloging-in-Publication Data
Names: Lichtenberg, Joseph D., author. | Thielst, Diana, author.
Title: From autism and mutism to an enlivened self : a case narrative with
    reflections on early development / Joseph D. Lichtenberg and Diana
    Thielst.
Description: Milton Park, Abingdon, Oxon ; New York, NY : Routledge,
    2019. | Series: Psychoanalytic inquiry book series | Includes
    bibliographical references and index.
Identifiers: LCCN 2018031156 (print) | LCCN 2018041748 (ebook) |
    ISBN 9780429432354 (Master) | ISBN 9780429778742 (Web PDF) |
    ISBN 9780429778735 (ePub) | ISBN 9780429778728 (Mobipocket/
    Kindle) | ISBN 9781138362000 (hardback : alk. paper) | ISBN
    9781138362017 (pbk. : alk. paper) | ISBN 9780429432354 (ebk)
Subjects: LCSH: Autism in children—Case studies. | Autistic children—
    Rehabilitation—Case studies. | Parents of autistic children—Biography.
Classification: LCC RJ506.A9 (ebook) | LCC RJ506.A9 L533 2019 (print) |
    DDC 618.92/85882—dc23
LC record available at https://lccn.loc.gov/2018031156

ISBN: 978-1-138-36200-0 (hbk)
ISBN: 978-1-138-36201-7 (pbk)
ISBN: 978-0-429-43235-4 (ebk)

Typeset in Times New Roman
by Swales & Willis Ltd, Exeter, Devon, UK

Contents

Introduction

What is autism, Asperger's, the syndrome, being on the spectrum? According to Oliver Sacks (1995), no two people with these designations are the same in form or expression. As we will illustrate with Anna, the autistic traits interact with adaptive often creative capacities and qualities. Sacks concludes that *if we hope to understand the autistic individual, a total biography is required.* Following this recommendation, we present Dr. Thielst's biography of her daughter, Anna, a little girl with autism who at age five didn't speak or answer to her name. For a biography of Anna to be meaningful, it must include the deep emotional story of her mother, Dr. T, and an account of those who worked with Anna to become a richly enlivened self – and those who criticized, shamed, blamed, and hindered. It is a story of dread and hope. Dread in the serious possibility that a talented little girl would remain lost in a world of confusion about human relatedness. Hope in that a way could be found by a determined innovative mother to bring her daughter into a world of mastery, language, and confidence. It is a story of failure and success. Failure for Dr. T after years of repeatedly seeking to find professional help that would even begin to penetrate Anna's wall of withdrawal and isolation. Success in Dr. T's leaving her country to consult experts in St. Petersburg who showed the way to open Anna's interest in responding and learning from others. It is a story of blindness and recognition. Blindness by family members to Dr. T's motherly sensitivity and determination and to Anna's ability. Recognition by Dr. T alone that Anna, even in her language-less withdrawal state, was capable of organized complex play with and manipulation of inanimate objects (Lego), of categorizing non-human events, and responding to music. It is a story of paralysis and restored initiative. Paralysis in that Anna could make no use of the human world for either learning or experiencing intimacy, and

Dr. T initially could do nothing herself to get help to understand or ame-liorate Anna's aversive detachment. Initiative for Dr. T and for Anna. For Dr. T persistently seeking answers to the mystery of an autistic developmen-tal state without even knowing or being helped to know of its existence or meaning. And then demonstrating creative initiative via a step-by-complex step reparative regimen. Initiative for Anna who was born with an inability to seek relating to her mother (or anyone) finally experienced the dramatic emergence of an intense desire to discern what Donald Duck and his bud-dies were up to and saying to each other. It is a story of shame and pride. Shame and blame – terrible paralyzing humiliation, embarrassment, and condemnation of Dr. T as a failed mother. And shame for Anna as a wild weird child who rocked herself, ran away, made odd sounds, and didn't speak. Shame for Dr. T was vividly present in the contempt and disdain of her husband and his family while Anna experienced the corrosive effect of the rejection of others at first without a clue as to its meaning or cause and later gaining painful recognition that other children and some teachers regarded her as strange and inferior. Pride from every little, then bigger, and finally unexpectedly huge steps forward that Anna took to become a suc-cessful professional who loves dancing and relates emotionally to people. Like her mother, Anna is an enlivened self.

From Autism and Mutism to an Enlivened Self is written in two parts. The first part is a chronological presentation by Dr. T of her experience as mother – puzzled, disappointed, blamed – but determined and innovative – and the eventually successful facilitator for Anna to emerge from the disability of an autistic state to an energized productive adolescent and adult. Dr. T's presen-tation takes the reader by the hand and vividly describes how years after birth Anna and she become a her *and* me – an us, mother and daughter hand-in-hand, eye-to-eye. In unusual detail, Dr. T describes the step-by-step remedial efforts leading to Anna's learning language, to converse, and to be socially competent. Anna's comments enhance the narrative. In the second part, I inform the reader of the discovery of autism as a developmental disorder. For the reader to understand the impact of the problematic developmental path of autism, I present a description of adaptive development for comparison. This part includes a summary of research revealing the abilities and capaci-ties of both a full-term healthily relating neonate and a one-year-old infant. These summaries of abilities and capacities of the neonate and one-year-old are compared with the present or absent adaptations in infants with autism.

Joseph D. Lichtenberg

Part I

Anna

Chapter 1

From missing relationship at birth to missing name and language at age five

Birth

It is the third day after birth. Highly complicated birth. Finally, we meet. A nurse hands her to me. Mentions something about the redness from forceps all across left cheek. Says not to worry – that it will disappear soon. Everything will be fine in just no time. She has very good weight, has recovered during these days apart from me and is now ready to meet with me. I am really not worried about her cheek. But I am worried. Worried about the trauma at birth. About the lack of oxygen. About the Apgar score of 4. Forceps. I somehow know deep inside that serious difficulties lie ahead. I feel it. I can think of cerebral palsy, epilepsy, all the developmental conditions I have learned in medical school – in a month I am going to be awarded a medical degree. For the majority of the medical students, both female and male, getting married and having their first child during the last couple of years of studies has been a norm for decades. It has been of particular significance for female medical students since it has been found much easier to give birth during the last couple of years of the six-year medical program than during any other time after the graduation. As a practicing doctor, the responsibilities and decision making for patient care on a daily basis could seriously interfere with the demands of pregnancy, birth, and the postpartum period. Being a medical student or a young doctor in a country with a high rate of female doctors, in a society where female doctors have been dominating the medical field for decades, means that getting married and having the first child at the same age as others outside the medical field – before the age of 25 – has been seen not just as being a normal part of the human experience, but encouraged by the medical faculty itself. So, here I am, meeting my first child while getting ready to take the Hippocratic oath in less than two months where I will swear "I will use treatment to help the sick according to my ability and judgment" and "May I long experience the joy of healing those who seek my help."

I take her to my chest. She starts crying. Does not stop. Screaming. With such a force. The nurse tries to help to soothe her, to adjust her on my breast. She just cries and cries. Finally, the nurse brings a bottle to her and starts to feed her while holding her. The whole situation changes in a fraction of a second. She immediately grasps the nipple of the bottle and starts to suck. Very actively. Suddenly, everything seems to normalize for her when the bottle is in the picture. She wants a bottle, not me. It feels that she seems not to recognize me. Not to know me at all. I feel guilty. This is our first meeting. And it feels like we are strangers. I believe that the trauma experience at birth has damaged not just both of us physically, but also the bond between us. The very same bond we were supposed to have been granted from nature.

First year

During the next months, and I don't know it yet but actually it's for years, nothing really changes regarding the relationship between us. It truly remains similar as it was during our first meeting. She refuses breastfeeding forever. Screams so loud. Wants a bottle instead. Bottle feeding has an immediate soothing effect on her. Nothing or nobody seems to be able to change this.

Then it becomes apparent that she doesn't want to be held either. Always prefers to be put down. Screams, arches her back. Calms down immediately when put down into her crib. Then I realize that she avoids looking at my face (or anybody else's face) – she looks always at something else – bottle, or toys. I realize I am more like an object for her, an object that gives her something so she can enjoy herself together with that object. She is a very beautiful baby. For many people she seems so brave, always knowing what she wants. And what she wants is always *something, not someone.* She doesn't seem to miss me when I leave, and is always busy with something when I return. Other people tend not to notice what I know from the beginning – she actually doesn't relate to me or anyone else.

However, the primary worry during the first months is that her motor development is seriously lagging. When at two months I take her to be evaluated by a child neurologist, she is unable to hold her head when lifted up. The lack of social smile is not even considered a primary issue when her motor development is not happening. Her general muscle tone is so weak. She doesn't respond with her body in any way when her position is changed. However, this "lagging motor development" seems not to affect all her motor actions like the sucking of a bottle or crying – these are strong, loud, and purposeful. She knows when she wants to eat and demands it very actively. Also, she is very vocal about her diaper change and demands it immediately and very loudly wherever we are. Her demands about her physical wellbeing are strong and seem not to correlate with her "weak muscle tone" in other situations like holding her head up when she should. When her needs for food, drink, diaper change are met, she seems happy in her crib or in her stroller. She sleeps generally well, gains weight as expected. Likes baths. Just trying to hold her is a problem – she typically cries with a very loud voice for a long time and doesn't stop before she is put down. Holding her has no soothing effect, it is not a way to stop her crying.

We begin with an intensive physical therapy program that includes movements, massages, swimming. As a result, she improves physically and catches up with other children her age. By six months, she is sitting up by herself. Standing at seven months and walking before her first birthday. Surprisingly rocking left to right in her crib when able to stand already. Rocking rhythmically and vocalizing with matched rhythm and beat: "aa – aah aa-aah." Looks like singing and dancing. But no social smile or eye contact, no reacting to her name, no first meaningful word yet. Reciprocity has not developed in parallel with her motor development. Despite having been surrounded by many family members in addition to me: her father, grandparents, uncles and an older very warm and attentive nanny, her behavior has been the same with everyone.

12 months

Around her first birthday, she seems a generally well-developed child. Her motor development is good. Walking, running. Active. I want to believe that the developmental issues are behind us. But deep inside I know that something is still very wrong. When she fails to react to her name at a time when other children do, I am not surprised. Others tend to think that she just doesn't want to respond since she is busy. This is how it looks. But I sense something more – that she doesn't know that she has a name. It seems to me that she doesn't know that she can be called by her name, or that she is expected to respond to it. Her name seems to have no significance for her. Like looking into people's eyes seems to mean nothing for her.

It is more than just not knowing her name or not making eye contact. She seems not to know that people relate to each other, that they share their feelings, and that they communicate with each other. She is so active all by herself and seems not to need anyone. Clearly, just calling her more often or more loudly doesn't do anything to catch her attention or make her want to join me or anyone else doing anything together. She is always too busy with something. Something so much more important to her. The most puzzling is that despite her lack of reciprocity in emotional interaction with me, when she is playing with her toys she seems to be an active well-developed typical child. She is vocalizing a lot using various pitches. It sounds like music. My mother keeps telling me that she is going to talk very soon. This is her feeling when she is observing her running around with toys in her hand and entertaining herself. Most people who know her see only the latter side of her. I am trying to express my concern, but I am told by many that mothers tend to see all kinds of problems in their children that in reality don't exist. That this is just mother's exaggerated worry that I am showing. I don't know what is wrong, but I do know that something is definitely wrong. And I don't know what to do about it. But I am on alert.

At 18 months she enters preschool. Generally, she looks like most other children in their development, except that when she is dropped off, she doesn't cry or miss me. I am told during the first days that she is doing very well – she is not crying and she is active by herself. That she is walking around trying to get food from the table before the actual mealtime begins when other children are still playing with toys. The preschool has the best early childhood educators. All with master's degrees. The best environment – an extraordinary building designed and built specifically for preschool. A lot of room, natural light, educational toys, speech stimulation, potty training, story times, singing, dancing, playing inside and outside. The best food from their own kitchen cooked freshly three times each day and served at a communal table using porcelain china. Eating being a part of education where children so early learn how to behave at the table. Sleeping in specially built wooden beds. Educators talk with each parent when they come to pick their children up around 4:30 p.m. each day. They talk about how each child has been that day. They talk about how to continue developing speech, empathy, potty training – all they did during the day – at home.

24 months

Her second birthday. Six months in preschool and no meaningful vocabulary yet. She is actively babbling by herself when running around and being constantly busy. I am trying to speak to her. The other family members do too. The preschool teachers do – where she is from 8:30 a.m. to 4:30 p.m. each weekday. The teachers start telling me that she has not said any words yet, in contrast to other children whose speech is already clearly developing. It feels that they seem even guilty that they have been not able to get her to start speaking. Also, they keep telling me that she doesn't sleep during the day like other children do. That they have to keep her from waking up other children who all do sleep.

Remarkably, despite her active babbling with high pitched voice and various rhythmic variations, her vocalizations have not turned to any meaningful communications. These seem to be directed just for herself. Like rocking from one leg to another looks like she is entertaining herself. There seems to be no difference who takes care of her – she is the same under everybody's care. Her behavior begins to clearly differ from other children. The normalization of her physical development – muscle tone, walking, running – has not led to improvements in her ways interacting with others. In some ways she is so advanced compared to others – fully potty-trained without any problem, eating and dressing by herself. Even doesn't need to sleep during the day like other children do. But when others are interacting with each other when they play, she has her own play without a need to look into anyone's eyes or interact in any way. When other children like their parents to help them get dressed when they are picked up, then she seems so advanced that she does it mostly by herself. At home, she goes to the refrigerator to eat by herself without making any attempt to ask for food when she is hungry. She is clearly very aware of her physical needs. But she seems to avoid being touched so much that she prefers to learn complicated motor actions so she doesn't have to depend on me or anyone else. She begins to look more and more alone compared with others who relate to each other. She is always busy with herself. Never coming to me or anybody else for any reason, always running away instead. When picking her up, and trying to hold her, she quickly finds a way to slide herself out of it. We are still trying to stimulate more, and wait for speech to suddenly appear.

30 months

The first visit to a speech therapist

I cannot wait any longer. I am making a decision, despite everyone else's waiting for her to suddenly speak. I want her to be evaluated and treated. I want to learn how to teach spoken language to her – to a child whose language clearly is not developing in a natural way. I want theory and guidelines. I expect to get all the knowledge of how it is done in a case like hers. I expect to get information about the books, workbooks, developmental toys, exercises. I need a full program. So that I can start immediately. I know somehow that I am the one who is supposed to teach language to her, not a speech therapist or educator. I even cannot imagine that someone else can teach language to her at this point. It certainly cannot happen during the speech therapy sessions a couple of hours per week. She is not interested in interacting with a speech therapist. Or an educator. Or me. I somehow realize that language can develop only through a relationship. Through that which is missing. So, I want to learn how to create this relationship, so that the beginning of language learning can take place. I am somehow convinced that it can be guided by a speech therapist, but actual work has to be done by me, the closest person to her. We have had a relationship before birth at least. How to get back to what I believe had been lost during the traumatic birth.

I make an appointment with a speech therapist specializing in children. Recommended by a child neurologist. I have high expectations. I need help from a language specialist, who knows everything about language development. I just need to have an appointment to get started. Ready to listen to what, where and how. Ready to work with her as long as necessary. So that we can overcome whatever we are facing here.

We enter the office. She is very friendly. Makes a great connection. With me. Talks – to me. Tries to get the attention of my daughter, who is running around. Tries again. Many times. It does not happen. She interprets it as just being in an unfamiliar situation. She seems to feel somewhat uneasy that she is not able to catch her attention. I say that it is always like that – with me, too. This information seems to mean nothing. She instructs me just to talk to her, show picture books to her, talk about what is happening in the picture. She is going to listen and start learning language and then talk. This is how it's done. This is how language develops. Through talking to a child. And verbalizing what is happening in the picture.

Some children start to talk later she says. I seem to know better already. I know that her language has not been developing. That is why I am here with her. I came to see her not for hope, but for guidance in the area that is not my specialty. My expectation for this consultation was to learn how language *can* be developed when it does not happen in a natural way. I came to learn about speech therapy "technique" that I thought existed, and apply it to everyday life for her. What I had not realized was that there was no speech therapy "technique" without preexisting speech and preexisting relationship.

We leave. Without a program, books, workbooks. Just with a recommendation to talk, talk, talk. But nothing really changes. For the next three years. Despite numerous visits to all kinds of specialists. And attempts to talk.

For the next six months everything stays very much the same. She shows no interest in looking at pictures in a picture book whether by herself or together with me as the speech therapist suggested, and no interest in paying attention to the description of pictures. She has been avoiding anyone's physical proximity, how is it even possible to make her sit with someone and look peacefully at the pictures in a picture book that she has no interest in? How can her language start developing in a setting where all components to make it happen – enjoyment of close physical proximity, sharing of emotions, content that is interesting to her – are missing?

She still doesn't respond to her name. Her expressive speech is limited to a few single word approximations, no attempts to combine these into phrases or sentences. No interest in doing anything together. What she keeps doing is being active by herself, running around and babbling. Like before. She does not stop her activities in order to talk or share in any other way what she has been doing or plans to do. However, she may pause her left-to-right rocking in order to vocalize rhythmically organized simple sound patterns for her own amusement. She seems to avoid any attempts to communicate with me – eye contact, physical contact, emotional contact. I don't know whether she is happy or not. I can only guess – she doesn't look sad for sure. She seems pleased with herself, focused on her own undertakings.

"Look into my eyes" – I keep telling her. Some people feel offended that she doesn't look into their eyes when they talk to her. Like she is disrespecting them. Why doesn't she look into anybody's eyes? I am holding her and making her look into my eyes. "Repeat the word" I say. She may even say that word after intense attempts. She may even know that this word means that particular object. And then she seems to do everything in her power not to say it again. Or say any other previously "learned" word again. These words that in other children develop into phrases and sentences keep disappearing as if they never existed. For her, words seem to be meaningless. The only clear communication seems to be running away from communicative attempts. Does she store any words in her memory at all? I am worried, but many of my close family feel just offended by her and begin to look at her as a "spoiled child" who is allowed to do everything, and who has therefore failed to learn to behave appropriately.

Getting no help from a speech therapist, and feeling guilty about her behavior, I realize how lonely I am. There is something I cannot communicate to anyone. That I am primarily worried about something that nobody else is worried about – the missing relationship. The bond that is supposed to always exist between a mother and a child. A continuous feeling between a parent and a child that they belong together. Always. That they light each other up with joy over and over again every single day. A feeling that I as a parent am the one she would reach out to when sad or insecure. That back and forth and simultaneous mimicking each other's actions that are so natural in a parent–child relationship. The reciprocity in our relationship is missing. We may have only minimal back and forth communication if at all. Emotionally, it would be much easier for me to go along with everybody else and pretend otherwise. So, it is really painful for me to be honest with myself and acknowledge it, but it is impossible for me not to notice it – it's like the continuous awareness, feeling, nonverbal communication that exists between musicians when they play together – a feeling I know so well since early childhood performing in various music ensembles. This is what is lacking. Her lack of language and unusual behavior seem to be a result of a lack of emotional connection. She regulates her emotions with her rocking and running around, not through me helping her. Without acknowledging the lacking relationship with others – the most basic issue in any child's development – I cannot see how anything can be done about it, how any intervention can be truly successful. I know already that just talking to her is not going to lead to speech development. That just talking to her is not going to create that bond. The bond is not about language but about feelings. How can I force her to look at my face, miss me when I am not there, react with pleasure when I come? How can I make her understand that she has a name? To make her want to say a meaningful word instead of vocalizing utterances mostly for herself? I don't recall anything like this from my medical studies. I don't recognize the syndrome. I cannot explain it from the viewpoint of the functional anatomy of brain, including Broca and Wernicke areas that are responsible for both understanding speech and motor aspects of speaking. I cannot explain it just from what is known about the role of hearing in speech development. What she has is larger than that. What is it?

36 months

Her third birthday. Still no spontaneous meaningful words despite a lot of vocalizations. "Aah – aah, eeh – eeh, eh-eh-eh-eh eeh." With various rhythmic patterns. Still mostly high pitched. Why don't these turn into communicative words and phrases? Why have none of the words she has repeated turned into word combinations, and phrases? Why does she seem to "forget" the "words" she has been "taught"? Still not responding to her name. Rocking her body from side to side, or a head from side to side has become a routine. The same behavior, but different age. Running actively around inside and outside continues. Avoidance of human interaction continues. Doesn't want to listen to anybody's instructions, directions, praise. Not verbal or otherwise. Sleeps six hours per night and does not sleep during daytime, unless she rocks herself for such a long time that she literally falls to sleep.

However, she is playing by herself and seems to enjoy herself when playing. Lines up toys, organizes them into circles and in many other systematic ways. She seems to work a lot. By herself and for herself. Others make accusations and blame me that go beyond that I have "spoiled my child." Accusations pour in from the same people who had previously told me not to worry. So many have been involved in her care and nobody has been able to "teach" her behavior or language that stays and leads to further development. Someone has to be blamed. It cannot be father or grandparents; it must be mother – me.

Finding the term "autism" when looking for answers from the literature

Disappointed that the speech therapy I had hoped would bring a difference did not fit her condition, I decide to do research on what speech patholo-gists study at the university, particularly, what is known about the initial stages of language development. I go to the university library and look through a lot of textbooks. Trying to find what is taught to the speech pathology students about how language of infants develops before the first word, and what does it mean when a child doesn't learn language in a natu-ral way – from her mother. What I find is that the content in the language acquisition literature seems to have very little relevance with the situation we have. None of the language development books seems to cover the topic I am interested in – how a child naturally learns the basic meaningful vocabulary and phrases, and how to address it when this doesn't happen in a natural development. No wonder that we have been not able to get any help from speech therapists – it is clearly not in their textbooks.

I keep looking. I try another library and bookstores specializing in medical literature.

Finally, I end up with a book about childhood aphasias. I quickly browse through pages right there in between the shelves before buying. It describes the conditions of motor and sensory aphasia, and other types of developmental language impairments.

This book is intended for medical professionals. It provides information about how different aphasias present from the neurological point of view, but not about how to deal with them. My daughter seems to have all these aphasic syndromes combined. Both motor and sensory. Both receptive and expressive language. But even these don't explain that missing bond between us. The situation we are having goes beyond words.

Then in the middle of a chapter discussing sensory aspects of childhood aphasias, I notice a word "autism" mentioned with the explanation of the Greek origin "autos" – self in the brackets. That's it! There is nothing more discussed other than children with autism also may not develop language. But the word itself "autism" – "self" – living in one's self, that is what fits what I have been looking for. I don't know anything about Leo Kanner's description or the Ivar Lovaas intervention model yet. Or that it may be impossible to get over this condition. The only thing I know is that the word "autism" describes best what I am facing with her. She is socially living in her own world, sharing her lived experiences with herself, communicating with herself, providing safety through rocking routines for herself. I am an outsider.

Since I don't know anything more about what "autism" may mean, and there is no internet yet, I don't have an easy access to the published literature as we have today. But I have my own understanding that when a child is living socially in his/her own world without the bond with parents, the first thing to do would be to try to create that bond. That would be not possible when she goes to preschool every single day. She is away for the whole day, the whole time away from an opportunity to establish a bond with parents. Despite that the preschool offers a safe and nurturing environment with developmental activities both inside and outside, and good freshly cooked food. Despite all this high quality early preschool experience, something is missing. The most basic thing is missing – a bond with mother and father. She is missing the basics.

Pulling her out of preschool

I decide, just me, the one blamed for the situation, that the first thing to do is take her out from preschool. So that I can create opportunities for her to be with me as much as possible. To accompany me wherever I go. So that she could possibly learn that me and her belong together, or at least have a chance to learn. So that she would possibly feel my presence, or at least have a chance to feel. So that through establishing myself as her partner throughout every single day she would have an opportunity to learn to relate to me. I cannot imagine how would it be possible to create a bond between me and my child by somebody else and without me. How can a specialist in any child development related field apply any kind of developmental technique on a child without getting parents involved, and expect that his/her intervention will result in creating a bond between a parent and a child – the bond that the whole life depends on? I take a lot of criticism for my decision to pull her out of preschool that anyone but me seems to understand. For me, it's about creating opportunities to build a foundation for her development – a strong parent–child bond – instead of trying to develop her just assuming without questioning that it exists.

I would take her every morning to my clinic where I oversee the health-care of the people in the area we live. While I am seeing patients, she is under the supervision of a nice outgoing middle-aged lady in a room down the hall from my office. She is continuously provided 1:1 attention while I am nearby. The lady makes sure that she physically stays inside, tries to draw together with her, play all kinds of games, engage her emotionally both to entertain her and keep her from running away. However, it happens over and over again that she is suddenly running into my office while I am seeing a patient or is caught on her way out of the building. It takes tremendous effort to just keep her in the room. However, the two do seem to form a kind of relationship. I, on the other hand, start feeling more and more guilty that I have not enough time for her. In this setting I can see it in a very profound way. I should be with her, but I can't. The most guilt kicks in when I realize that during the time while I am being fully involved in patient care, I may temporarily forget all about her. It starts tearing me apart more and more – two worlds that both require 100 percent of me simultaneously. In addition to being a wife and a daughter-in-law expected to keep a tidy home, entertain guests, and provide a welcoming and warm home environment to everyone.

My patients get used to her around, and many times they come with a candy or a toy for her, creating an extra opportunity for communication. Although I am under enormous pressure that drains both my physical and emotional energy, I do feel that she gets used to me being around as somebody who belongs with her. This is why I keep going. I don't see an alternative. I have to work, and she has to be with me – what else can I do other than try to combine these whatever the cost to my own wellbeing. Progress seems very slow, invisible to others, and a concern for me. Speech doesn't develop as a result of it. I am looking for more opportunities to bond with her.

Her fourth birthday

No significant change in language. At this age her behavior looks very different from other children of the same age. It looks like it has a wild component in it. It is not acceptable behavior at four years of age and I know it. Only one thing seems to be clear: there is no reason to believe or even hope, that somehow, miraculously, she will be growing out of this. Not behaviorally or language-wise. I realize that right now I can still run after her and pick her up to bring her to safety – her weight is of a four-year-old. How about teenage years? It is terrifying. A human being without socialization and language, and emotional regulation through connecting to others. Without a name. Without a wish to be with others, learn from them, and give something in return.

Wandering away from home or any other place when we are together on a daily basis becomes more prominent. Just leaves when we don't notice. Goes to the street and keeps going. "She is deaf – this is why she does not speak and behaves this way" or "She needs a very strong hearing aid so that she can hear" – I am told. It is only later when I figure out that she actually ends up in some silent place, including inside of the neighboring homes with unlocked doors. Since she is considered profoundly deaf by now by her father and her grandparents from her father's side – all musicians and music educators who seem to have an understanding that a life without the ability to hear is worthless – the sound environment at home becomes increasingly loud due to her father's daily experiments with high-intensity surround sounds. When the walls and floors shake as a result of very loud music, the environment that is intolerable for the majority of people, it cannot affect a "deaf" child as I am told every single time when I try to intervene. Clearly, we are no longer in the same boat regarding parenting. Her father with his parents behind him seems to have developed a dramatically different understanding about our daughter. The paternal grandparents' view is the following:

> a poor child whose mother doesn't do anything for her development, and whose father lets this happen being unable to take charge of the situation and his wife, a worthless medical doctor who is unable to treat her own child.

This pressure adds tremendous stress to an already existing situation – a child who doesn't develop language or socialization. With our daughter present, I hear with increasing frequency how useless my medical education is and that every single family friend we have pities *him*. As a result, every single day I feel I become more and more alone, that our daughter and I are as a pair of worthless individuals who cause so much trouble for *him* and *his* family. What *we* can do becomes what I *alone* can do to enhance our daughter's development.

But I am who I am. While it is extremely hard to be considered responsible for my daughter's failure to develop language and to control her behavior, not anyone, neither father or grandparents or disappearing family friends, can destroy me as a human being. Somehow I understand them. My hope is that I can change their attitudes once I figure out what to do.

Seeing a child neurologist

I take her to my child neurology professor for evaluation and advice what to do. Her father doesn't show any interest in seeing a child neurologist and declines a suggestion to be present during the visit. So it is just me and our daughter. We enter my professor's office and start discussing her development. She runs out of the doctor's office and I have to go catch her and bring her back. No play, no interaction, just wild behavior. I mention the word autism. I learn that the university child neurology department has no experience in autism or a similar condition. They don't know how to diagnose or intervene. They can only exclude other conditions, which they do. My professor tells me that I have to start immediately socializing her. What is clearly seen is that there is no socialization at age four. The main attention seems to be not at the lack of language, but at the lack of socialization. This is how she presents. But how to socialize her – nobody knows. I am expected to find out myself and also educate the doctors. I deeply appreciate the honest expertise from my professor – I realize that it takes the highest level of expertise to be able to say "I don't know." Also, it is the first professional decision I can sincerely appreciate.

More than ever it becomes clear that it does not make sense to try another speech therapist, another medical test, teacher, method. Without experience there is no true specialist in existence. A speech therapist or special educator who has never developed speech in a speechless child with behavior problems cannot possess the professional skills necessary for meaningful evaluation or effective intervention for my child. I had been wondering why none of these "specialists" agreed to discuss any aspects of language development at the brain level with me. They just kept turning me down one after another without even entering into discussion. The message was "they are specialists and know everything about child development and I am not." So I should believe them without questioning. But how can I ever trust anyone to predict my child's future who refuses to talk with me about brain and language development, the most direct issue related to my child's development and future? My daughter needs more than just a support system. She needs the whole system where all aspects of development are integrated. So, finally receiving the conclusion "We don't have experience" from my child neurology professor is truly refreshing. It would have been much easier if also speech therapists and other professionals would have been able to distinguish between what they know and what they don't. My daughter is already four. Other children her age will soon learn to read, write, do math, and enter school. We have only a couple of years to come up with a solution to catch up. This is my inner voice telling me to act quickly. Also, being aware of the advantage of early intervention from the neuroplasticity point of view, we don't have much time anyway. I have had the feeling all along that she is able to develop when someone can figure out how. That someone has narrowed down to me alone.

Starting to look for a way out: what can she do and what could it mean?

Putting aside my own feelings, I start fresh by looking at her in a systematic way. I know what she can't do. But what about her strengths? What *can* she do? What are her intellectual capabilities despite her lack of language? At which level can she theoretically lead her life when her abilities are all developed into their maximum capacity?

After realizing that she did not start to speak "suddenly and miraculously," most people who know her seem to be under the impression that she is not able to make any sense of the surrounding world. It seems so easy to judge that she does not understand anything when there is no language. However, although she may look like she lives in her own world for most of the time, she seems to have an ongoing connection with her visual and motor experiences. She likes to dress herself, chooses only soft comfortable clothes, and matches her outfits by color and style.

What could this mean? Clearly, she knows her body; she is able to sort her clothes according to their function, appearance, and comfort;

she knows where different clothes belong in relation to her body; she has enough motor planning to end up fully dressed.

Also, she likes to line up and organize toys into a variety of geometrical shapes. Even though it may look like an odd and unusual way of playing for many, she must have noticed these shapes somewhere, and stored them in her memory. Furthermore, she has built a beautiful house from Lego pieces with a very well-constructed red roof with a ridge on top of it, blue walls, white windows and a yellow door – all the parts in appropriate relation to each other in size and location.

What could this mean? Obviously, she has learned from somewhere that there are parts that make a whole. She must have noticed the different colors in the environment. And then, she somehow has figured out how to put them all together.

Against all odds, based on her wild behavior, lack of language, and odd play, she must be able to think constructively. And this is not a low level thinking. Moreover, her fine motor skills have developed enough to connect Lego pieces with each other to build a house. Initiating, identifying, recognizing, comparing, categorizing, blending, retrieving from memory, creating, planning, executing seem all to be included in her play. The same play where nobody else but she is participating. A little girl who is considered by so many to be detached from the world and so incapable.

Her hearing doesn't make sense

What about her auditory experiences? I start by weighing thoroughly what I have noticed about her reactions to sounds and how these observations can be interpreted from the medical point of view.

Since she does not respond to her name and has not developed language, she has been considered deaf by many people, an opinion prevalent among the general public and professionals alike. *"Nobody can shout so loud that she can hear"* – I am told. *"The strongest hearing aids for both ears should have been provided a long time ago"* – I am told. All based on pure tone behavioral audiometry, the main hearing test at a time. But the pure tone thresholds for "profound" hearing loss are in a similar range with auditory pain thresholds. Are the results the thresholds for pain or auditory acuity? The audiometry is extremely hard to perform in a child who is never still and pays no attention to those quiet pure tones coming from the earphones she doesn't like to wear. The pure tones are certainly novel sounds to her, since they do not exist naturally in the environment, and they sound very unpleasant to anybody when played loud enough. The sound of a single frequency alone doesn't have timbre – it's not a speech sound and it's not a musical sound, just a mechanical sound event without any communicative or emotional value. What can the behavioral responses to these few emotionless pure tone frequencies in the speaking range truly mean, the setting that never occurs in a natural environment? How to explain "profound hearing loss" in the presence of her modulated voice that everyone can observe – the voice quality that deaf individuals have to be specially trained to achieve to some extent. How to explain that she tends to cover her ears with her hands frequently? What is she hearing so unpleasant with her "profound" hearing loss, that has to be protected by covering her ears?

How did she hear those words she repeated after me when she didn't hear them? How did she match the pitches and melodic contours of the words she repeated after my singing and change the musical key exactly like I did – a set of words in pitches in one musical key, and the same set of words in another, and then the third musical key? My ability to detect the exact pitches of sounds – absolute pitch – enables this observation easily. I am unaware that any audiologist, speech therapist, special educator, music therapist or any other professional has ever reported – whether in a child whose language development is not happening or any in an individual of any age with any communication issue. This observation is critical for her development since it shows she has an ability to not just notice, but also memorize these sounds with such a precision that enables her to retrieve from her memory and produce an exact imitation of both the pitches themselves and their sequences. The words seem to mean nothing for her but the sounds themselves seem to have a different relationship with her. It can be easily tested, but before that, someone has to consider this as an important component of auditory processing and spoken language acquisition, and develop a way to communicate through sounds before switching to words. What could be the significance of this observation when she is considered and tested as profoundly hearing impaired at the same time?

Also, how did she hear my violin playing, even from far away – long hallway and two doors closed in between? The same for my piano playing. An individual with a profound hearing loss cannot hear that. It is physically impossible. Moreover, she liked my violin playing, but hated loud and fast Chopin's etudes and waltzes, and occasional Beethoven that I used to play so much that she ran to me repeatedly clearly upset and using gestures demanded that I stop playing. For me it says that she is able not just to hear from far away but knows the difference in instrumental timbres, and that she has been attaching different emotions to these timbres.

Interestingly, when she makes a sound herself, she seems to be always aware of it. Does it mean that when she expects sounds as a result of her own action, she can hear these immediately? Or even more, how is it possible that she responds to my violin playing being in her room down the hallway with two doors closed in between, and can't hear enough to develop spoken language? Her hearing responses do not make sense at all.

How is she supposed to learn language when she shows no interest in sharing thoughts and feelings in any form of communication except responding to my violin and piano playing? How can I use the information from my observations about her to develop reciprocity in our relationship, learn language, and change her behavior, so she can become a contributing member of society? How can her speech be developed using these observations about her unrecognized relationship with sounds when she has no interest in looking at pictures in children's picture books and talking about them as recommended by a speech therapist? I come to the realization that in the field of raising a child there isn't anything that works for her. She is so different. She operates in her own way in the world without the need to share it with anyone.

Exposing her to different environments as the first learning tool

I am coming to the decision to make my own plan about how to proceed. How to provide the opportunities for the most optimal development for her? Which developmental aspects should be chosen as the most basic to be addressed, which would possibly affect several other processes in addition? My plan is to reorganize my life to keep her next to me for as long as possible during the day. Me and her. Belong together. Always. But what else?

It seems to be obvious at this point, that without language she can learn only from her immediate environment. Other children her age learn both through their own experiences, and through listening and talking about the experiences of others. These all add up for learning proposes. She has only the immediate environment to learn from. Therefore, going to different places as frequently as possible becomes very important for her development. Providing her with new opportunities for a variety of experiences by changing environments would enable her to access more information about the world than staying within the same surroundings. We all need novelty to keep us attentive and interested. For her, going to places may mean the only way to get in touch, and learn about the outside world. She does not have the same freedoms as others. Lack of language and nonexistent interest in communication can easily lead to a very limited world experience when we don't address it. Despite lack of language and communication, she can be provided with ways to develop in a nonverbal way, so that her strengths can develop further.

Changing environments would mean an opportunity for stimulation and information. New sights, sounds, smells, tastes, and a variety of combinations of all of these. It would mean exposure to new physical objects with numerous features, and an opportunity to recognize the familiar ones. It would mean exposure to events, where things happen in time, with beginning and end. When playing inside by herself, she is focused on lining up toys. What about learning to focus outside, in another environment? Going just out to a store while I shop, for example, would position her in a passive mode, and easily end up with behavior problems. But what about letting her choose items in the grocery store? In her play she makes choices between clothes, Lego pieces of different colors, toys, she picks them up and organizes them. Similarly, she should be able to choose and pick up items in the store for purchase.

I choose a small local grocery store. I choose a day and a time when only a few people are expected to do shopping. I let her go around by herself, while I observe her from a distance, ready to get to her at any moment. She walks down the aisle, stops here and there, looks at the items on a shelf and seems to think. And then she makes a decision. Picks a pack of candy from the shelf, then two more. Soon she finds herself at the cashiers, three packs of candy in her hands. I step in for payment. We go outside, she opens one of the packs and enjoys the taste of that candy. The same candy she had just bought by *herself*. The type of candy *she* had chosen from the shelf out of many options. She seems happy. She seems important. She has just discovered a way to make a wish come true. Through action. Through choice and decision. Through an opportunity to make it happen. She learns a word – "store." This word does not disappear like it never existed. It becomes a symbol.

Swimming pool. Indoor. A group lesson for mothers and children her age or little older. Water environment. Among other children. Every child with their own mother. I am holding her strongly when we enter the full size pool. The water touches the skin all over her. She seems to be aware of the change from the air environment into the water environment. She seems to feel it on her skin. Wet. Deep water. When I would put her down, only her head would remain above the water level. She seems scared, holding me tighter and tighter with her hands and legs around me. I don't recall this feeling ever before. I am becoming her security. She never seemed to need me. She never put her arms and legs around me. But here she does. I become for the time in the pool her lifeline. I miss all of what the instructor says, a middle-aged woman with strict and demanding voice. I am connecting with my daughter, physically and emotionally. I let her a little loose and she clings back to me. Back to safety. I look into her eyes, which are so close to me right now, and say a word like "cat," "dog," "pool." She repeats immediately after me. Without hesitation. Many times. Saying words is so much easier in this situation.

We come back for another lesson. She seems to have trust in me this time. And time to notice other children. The instructor throws small heavy colorful toys into the water for each child, and then encourages them to bring these to her. Colorful toys from the bottom of the pool. It can be done only by going fully underwater with eyes open. One by one, other children get over their fears of diving, and show their pride to their mothers when they are returning to the surface, a toy in hand. We are holding each other and still trying to get our heads under the water together. During the third lesson, when the instructor throws a toy for my daughter, she goes after it. She goes fully under the water towards the bottom, but without getting a toy, comes back to the surface. She notices other children next to her. They are actively diving to get the toys from the bottom of the pool, and she decides to try again. Until she gets it. Finally, she comes to the surface, a yellow toy fish tightly in her hand and gives it to me while clinging to my body with her arms and legs around me. I am the one she returns to. I am the one she gives something. Up till now, it has been always the other way around. And now she returns to me from deep under the water like other children return to their mothers after their dive. Many concepts to become aware of. Wet and dry. Danger and safety. By herself and among other children. Fear and pride. Her own mother and other mothers. The social circle. In the water environment. Where understanding language or talking ability does not matter so much.

Home environment. Providing opportunities to enhance her play seems another way to ensure that her strengths can develop further. Endless new toy choices, new puzzles, new Legos, new Barbie sets, houses and dolls with full wardrobe. It seems that most of the developmental toys and puzzles available have ended up in our home. Going to toy stores becomes a frequent activity – I let her choose the toys she likes. And she seems to choose wisely.

One day she gets a chance to visit her grandmother's Orff orchestra for four-year-olds when she is under her care for a couple of weeks and the grandmother doesn't find a babysitter one day. The Orff approach is a developmental approach that combines elemental hands-on music making with language and movement using instruments like xylophones, drums, recorders, and the like. In an Orff orchestra, children learn to make music together. It is learning by doing in the music medium in the form of play where children have to respond and act within a predetermined musical meter – time. As in a swimming pool, it appears that she is a different child also here. Suddenly she likes to be with other children, to communicate through music making, playing the instruments, noticing her place among others, waiting for her turn to play a note. Most importantly, she seems to be aware of other children and a teacher, her grandmother, in the classroom. Connects with others via making sounds on the instruments. Waiting for her turn to do so. Orff music making with other children makes sense to her, she understands it. She is not wandering away from here. She is present and participating. Her grandmother is impressed but is afraid to take her for more lessons, since the parents of other children in this highly selected group of musically able four-year-olds may not like her among their kids. According to her grandmother, she doesn't belong among musically able kids. Where does she belong?

I realize that even though her grandmother finds this particular music classroom so beneficial for her granddaughter's development, she doesn't want her in her class. It starts to make sense to me why even music teachers, in this case an elementary music teacher who teaches a four-year-olds' class finds her own four-year-old granddaughter "not suitable" for music making although she had been "so good" according to her own assessment. I become fully aware that it is not about my daughter, her granddaughter. It is about herself, the grandmother, and her own feeling of being superior to other people. She is known in this small town for being highly offensive by telling parents how untalented their kids are and that there is no sense to develop them musically – they are hopeless. How could she accept her own granddaughter in her class then? She, who feels so important while being in charge of admissions for a four-year-olds' Orff class in the town. She would feel of lesser value if she would allow other children, those who are not supposed to be affiliated with her circle of highly selected children she agrees to teach, to join in. Even her own granddaughter's development doesn't break her feelings about herself. It is her identity. She can be "superior" only when "inferior" exists. She has a power to exclude. She cannot give this power away. Previously, I had been puzzled by her family's comments on Special Olympics, particularly winter sports – the whole family found it "terrible" to watch when individuals with disabilities compete in sports instead of staying home out of the public view. It all makes sense now. They cannot allow that "Special Olympics" to come into their music classes. They make sure that their music lessons, which would enable communication with other children, remain out of their "special" granddaughter's reach. I learn in a painful way that inclusion may be a true roadblock even within a family.

As usual, my daughter's positive behavior change that happened in her grandmother's Orff classroom – participation, attention, actions, communication –disappears soon after the lesson is finished. Nothing seems to stick. The connection with her happens but it seems to be more like playing a note on a piano, where the sound quickly fades after the hammer hits the string, unlike with a violin where a sustained sound is created by bowing a string.

Her fifth birthday

She is used to going places now. Grocery stores. Toy stores. Eating out in small cafeterias where she can choose what she wants from the display. Art galleries. Concerts. Swimming twice per week. Does not run away anymore. It is all easier due to her positive behavior change. Seems to be aware of her parents and grandparents now. We, me and her, are more like a team now, particularly when going out. Uses about 30 words or approximate words. Minimal language. Despite all my efforts, the 30 words she knows and uses purposefully still do not turn into phrases and sentences. Voice is high pitched. Demands expressed in one word. "Store" means that she wants to go to the store to buy something good for herself. She has said one sentence spontaneously so far – "frog went to store."

Most people who know her, do not see any change for the better. "Since she has been unable to develop spoken language, nothing else matters" – I hear, when I try to explain or show, that there are areas where she is doing very well like Lego building, complicated puzzles, swimming independently at age five. Most children her age learn more through talking, and interacting, while being less involved in building complicated Lego constructions or solving hard puzzles. Therefore, comparing her with other children makes sense only for language and social interaction. *Her* strengths and interests are thought not to matter. They are considered unimportant. The pressure to accept her as incapable for advancing in development grows. Many people are angry with me, accusing me of being a mother who is unfit for raising a child. There is no official diagnosis other than "profound hearing loss." There is no information where I am at that time that would enable an explanation of her atypical development. She is considered just "unteachable." It is early 1990s.

I have to agree, that in the area of language development, she shows no significant advancements. The advancements are all in other areas – creating Lego buildings, solving 300 and above piece puzzles, swimming 25 yards using breast strokes, diving, behaving in public, focusing in different environments. The intensive attempts to teach her language have resulted only in a small number of words or their approximations. Building joint attention has increased communicative attempts, but not language. Acquired words have not led to longer speech. Instead, they have become the shortest way to communicate a demand. No need for sharing. Only concentrating on how her wishes can become true. And they have grown bigger, and expensive. It looks like she just doesn't get the concept of spoken language – that people communicate with each other, because they like it, because they want to share, and learn from each other. Minimal physical and emotional communication in infancy seems somehow to be connected to minimal verbal communication at age five. Despite the remarkable advancements in many areas, the pressure to accept that she is unable to learn is enormous. It feels like everything we have achieved together must be considered to be worth nothing. According to other people. I see her significant internal learning potential without knowing how to turn it into language. Others don't agree and keep pressuring me not to see her strengths at all. It is tearing me apart. The fact is, her language *is* limited to 30 words at age five and a half. And I don't know how to teach it to her.

Losing her when the accusations take the worst turn

Although I have been trying harder and harder, the accusations, mostly coming from her father's family, intensify. Despite the numerous clear connections happening between us, there is still no language beyond single words or their approximations. And that shows. Everything she does well seems not to matter – there is still no language. I hear that I am a failure. Failed mother. Unable to teach her to talk. I hear that I am a failed medical doctor. Unable to treat her. I hear that my parental rights must be taken away and my medical incompetence regarding an inability to treat her reported.

One day it happens. She is taken away by her father's family and hospitalized to prove that her condition is due to deafness that her mother and everybody else involved have failed to detect. And that the only things she needs are two strong hearing aids for both ears to make her hear, so that language can develop.

I learn that behind this unusual hospitalization and unfortunate turn of events is a close family member from my daughter's father's side – an anesthesiologist, who had an otorhinolaryngologist as a close friend. The main purpose as I am told had been to "save the child from her incapable mother through determination of a correct diagnosis which is not possible with mother present." I don't know what to do. I cannot accept that I am nobody, and that all of it was planned behind my back. I am terribly alone. And helpless. It only gets worse.

Before I can figure out how can I prove myself to the system, and protect myself and my daughter, she is handed back to me. She did not accept the hearing aids. She covered her ears and ran away like in many other situations throughout the previous years.

One night, when she was still hospitalized, I walk home with a guest lecturer, a neurologist from St. Petersburg in Russia, who teaches a neurorehabilitation course I chose to attend to get my mind off the impossible situation, I find myself telling her about my daughter. I feel so unworthy and so terrified that I can hardly speak. She asks, and I answer. I am telling her about my daughter's lack of speech, and my lack of knowledge. It is a brief discussion. She responds that she knows somebody in St. Petersburg in Russia, who I may want to see. She may know how to make the contact happen, an important factor, since that person is usually unapproachable. I immediately pick up on it. I have been cornered. I have been made to feel worthless both as a parent and as a human being. I am in an impossible situation. I would look anywhere for anyone who can make sense of it. I would go anywhere to meet someone who knows something about children who don't acquire language and who have behavioral issues. So far, I have not been able to find anyone. I learn that this person in St. Petersburg to whom I have been recommended has retired lately, but that she still sometimes sees patients in her home.

Chapter 2

The four critical months before the sixth birthday

From learning her name to reading and from reading to learning to speak in 1000 hours

Meeting with Dr. Traugott

In a few weeks, the first week of January 1992, I am walking together with my five-year-old daughter up the stairs of a heavy building at Blochin Street, not far from the Gorki metro station in St. Petersburg. Her father is not with us. Just me and her. Her tendency to wander seems to be finally behind us, so I feel I can travel with her without worrying that she is going to run away when I don't notice. My attempts to keep her beside me for a period of two years have at least one positive outcome. I don't know what she is thinking or feeling – her vocabulary is still limited to about 30 single word-like vocalizations. But she looks peaceful and content. It's only 25 years later I learn about *her* experiences of that trip to St. Petersburg – that she remembers a church, a building, and how fascinated she was seeing a tram in the street that had a huge number "57" on, and that she had been so impressed by that large number since the only trams she had ever seen so far had only single digit numbers on them. Who would have thought what she was noticing and thinking since there was no language, and no wish to share her thoughts and feelings? I ring the bell. We are asked to wait for Dr. Traugott in her office, which looks like a library. I don't know much about the doctor we are to meet. I don't know her exact specialty other than she has a long-term experience with children who don't learn to speak. While we are waiting I notice the books on the shelves with titles in several languages. Brain. Neurophysiology. Neuropsychology. Freud. Consciousness. She enters the room. Her name is Natalya Nikolayevna Traugott.

She asks the first question – what is my daughter's name? I say her name. She asks another question – what is wrong with her? I respond with only one sentence: "She is not talking as she should." I am about to explain about her lack of speech, contradictory hearing responses, behavior that is so much better already, and her strengths in Lego building and puzzles. She is not interested in it at this point. She says she is going to examine her hearing in *her own way* first. She has developed her own method to evaluate hearing in children who don't learn to speak. Her method allows her to reveal crucial aspects of children's responses to sounds that are missed in conventional hearing tests. Her approach is not only critical for understanding a child's capacity to connect to surrounding sounds, but is also foundational for designing effective interventions. For the first time, a consultation with a doctor doesn't begin with talking but doing – with interacting with a child directly, instead of collecting information from parents.

Dr. Traugott places my daughter right in front of her, facing another direction so that she cannot see the doctor without turning her head. She says her name with a usual speaking voice right from behind her, not giving her an opportunity to see her speak. Just an auditory stimulus. Her name. No response. The doctor calls her louder. Then louder, and even more louder. No response. She is shouting her name. Still no response. She is shouting her name again. And finally, my daughter turns her head towards the doctor. Slowly. With a somewhat puzzled look in her face. The same in her body movement. Her eyes seem to meet Dr. Traugott's eyes. For a moment filled with both hesitation and true connection simultaneously. She is like "is it possible that someone wanted something from me? By making this noise? Was this noise directed to me?"

I don't recall anything like this before. Always, it has been running after her to give her something. Now, in front of my eyes, Dr. Traugott makes her pay attention to her via sound first, and only then she gives her something. Dr. extends her arm with a small piece of candy on her palm. My daughter responds immediately by taking the candy and eats it. During these few seconds, I see them truly communicate with each other. Purposefully. First, Dr. Traugott calling her by name, then she responding by looking towards her, then realizing that Dr. Traugott wanted to give her candy – that was what this noise must have been about, and finally, taking a candy from Dr. Traugott and eating it with pleasure.

Dr. Traugott calls her again with a softer voice, right from behind her like previously. Now she is responding immediately after the first try. She turns herself around quickly, without hesitation, without that puzzled look like before. Her eyes are meeting Dr. Traugott's eyes again. She seems to know already what this sound is about. Dr. offers her a piece of candy again. Her facial expression shows that she likes the taste of the soft yellow banana candy she is offered. This candy seems to be worth paying attention to. She seems to start expecting hearing the sound, her name, so that she can get the candy from Dr. Traugott again. She learns quickly that Dr. Traugott and candy go together. She doesn't get candy from a table or somewhere else after hearing the sound. It's always in Dr.'s palm, her arm extended towards her, her eyes looking at her, and a sound that leads to all of this. From sound to human interaction. The sound that becomes meaningful and another human being whose presence becomes meaningful for her through the connection via sound is her name.

Next, the doctor increases the distance between her and my daughter to about 3 feet, facing another direction like before, so that she cannot see who, where, and when the sound is coming from. The sound that connects her to someone. A sound pattern that lasts less than a second – her name. A sound pattern babies usually respond to by their first birthday and that connects humans to each other being among the first words used when people who don't know each other introduce themselves. A sound pattern that is part of each person's identity. Dr. Traugott calls her again. She responds immediately and gets a candy. Then 6 feet. Then 10 feet. 20 feet. She is responding fast and getting a piece of candy immediately. She has "learned" the game. She has developed from seemingly being profoundly hearing impaired – not responding to shouting her name just behind her ear – to a hearing individual who responds to her name from the distance of 20 feet without the opportunity to see who calls her. It is happening right here, in the doctor's home office. In my presence. But it is more than just about being able to hear and respond when she wants to. It's also about being able to make a connection with another human being when she wants to. There is a reason behind somebody calling her by name, and there is a reason why she responds. Underneath, there is a common interest, a purpose, a thought, expressed in sound without which spoken language wouldn't exist.

I am stunned – in less than half an hour, in front of my eyes, without any additional information, knowing just her name and "she does not speak as she should," Dr. Traugott identifies her core problem critical for understanding her behavior and lack of language. She does it in a way that displays my daughter's basic weakness: inconsistent responses to auditory stimuli. I have known it all along by observing her in different environments. She has been hearing the sounds of the violin and piano, but not responding to her name.

She has been responding to the birds singing but not somebody speaking next to her. She may respond to whispering but not to conversational speaking or shouting. Dr. Traugott spots my daughter's underlying problem – why she has not developed speech beyond these hardly acquired 30 words. That she responds to sounds only when she pays attention to them. She pays attention to sounds only when they convey meaning for her and for which she has previously developed an interest. She responds when she feels it is useful for her. When she has an interest in it. When she knows to expect it. When she can extract it from other sounds in the surrounding environment. When she can compare the sounds to the ones in memory. When she has been able to build a capacity for auditory memory and where to retrieve it. Dr. Traugott gets this information just by interacting with her, not from my explanations, imaging or any other medical tests, or standard questionnaires. 'Not responding to her name' becomes 'responding to her name' within 30 minutes.

As it appears, she *has* an ability to make eye contact; an ability to pay attention to other person; an ability to develop short-term memory necessary for language acquisition: a capacity to learn. It's all happening in this setting when being approached by a person who knows *what*, *when*, *how*, and *why*.

It is not "profound hearing loss," Dr. Traugott says. She can hear from 20 feet. She can physically hear enough of what is necessary for spoken language acquisition. But it is not enough that the speech or other auditory signals just enter her brain. She has to attach meaning to the speech and non-speech sounds. She has to associate the sounds and their patterns with meaning. She has to develop auditory memory, and without meaningful auditory stimulation, it cannot develop. This is where the impairment is. 'No meaning attached to sounds' means also 'no development of auditory memory capacity.' And this means no spoken language acquisition in a way most infants learn. When she is interested in what she hears, she employs her attention, including attention to sounds. Without interest, she pays no attention to sounds. Without understanding, there is no interest – native language sounds like a foreign language. There is no reason to pay attention to it. Learning to understand speech requires building auditory capacity for interpreting patterns of sound sequences that are highly variable in timbre, pitch, intensity, and loudness. Without this capacity language cannot develop via an auditory pathway.

Now we talk. Discuss. I learn more about Dr. Traugott. That she has personal interest in studying how auditory system is functioning in relation to lack of speech in children, and how language is organized in the brain.

From the beginning of the 1930s she continued the work of several professionals who had previously described children with behavior problems who didn't learn language despite having normal intelligence and hearing acuity. She has led a lab of evolutionary physiology. Studied consciousness. That she is a student of Pavlov, known across the world for his work in classical conditioning. And that they worked together until Pavlov's death in 1936. Both interested in combining medicine and education. And we discuss education. What can be done. She believes that people in the field of medicine, including neuropsychology, have to work together with people in education. It is not enough to recognize the syndrome and explain it. Working out trajectories for cognitive and other aspects of intervention is as important. The education field cannot work out effective interventions by themselves and without fully understanding a problem. When medical and psychology professionals have trouble understanding problems related to underdevelopment of language, then education professionals cannot develop effective educational interventions by themselves. How the auditory system works is not easy to understand. Different scientific areas must be combined. Interdisciplinary teamwork is the only way that can lead to the development of educational and therapeutic approaches that work. She explains that my daughter needs to learn language in a different way compared to how children usually acquire their native tongue. She has to be taught a native language as if it were a foreign language, under difficult conditions, when there is no native language to base it on. Her responses to sounds are uncertain, fluctuate. Language can't be learned that way – speech sounds change continuously. Her visual strengths must be used to their maximum capacity to speed up the learning. And weaknesses must be worked on. So I learn that it is possible to teach her. This is what matters to me the most right now – it can be done when done right.

Dr. Traugott stresses that the very carefully designed teaching system they have worked out has been effective, but only for these children whose close family members understand the processes involved. Understanding how auditory and visual systems work and how important it is to ignite an interest in a child for learning is necessary. Developing a strong emotional connection between a child and an adult responsible for developing a child throughout days, weeks, and months to come means building a foundation for everything else. Language development cannot happen without that. This is why family members are so important. Who else can get emotionally more connected to a child than those who love him or her? Who else can become a close partner with a child so that a stronger relationship can develop leading to communicating emotions both via nonverbal ways and promoting language use? Speech or any other therapy twice per week is not going to reach the true potential for these children long term. It's not about "applying a therapeutic method." It's about developing a child non-stop. It's about providing a child with tools that enable him or her to explore the world, access information out there, share the experiences with others and learn from others. Connecting, noticing, guiding, directing, changing directions, keeping a child's interests up, experiencing and sharing together. Providing visual ways to learn while working on attaching meanings to sound patterns that enable the development of an auditory system – a system that enables us make sense of the sound world around us and understand human interaction via spoken language. Communicating both nonverbally and verbally. Including thinking in all everyday activities. Conditioning and fading it immediately when not necessary. Dr. Traugott tells me about an 11-year-old boy with a similar condition whose mother is also a medical doctor. She has been personally developing her son who now is fluent not only in native language, but is learning a foreign language, is very much interested in geography, participates in a general classroom actively, con-tributes on a daily basis interesting facts for the whole class in a general classroom, so that other children are interested in learning from him in addi-tion to what is covered by the teacher. At this point it sounds more like a fairy tale to me – it is almost impossible for me to imagine that this level of literacy and functioning may one day fill the life of my daughter. However, I take a notice that a crucial factor in connecting with others is that she has to contribute socially in a way that they develop interest in her.

Surprisingly, Dr. Traugott, fluent herself in five languages, tells me not to be afraid of my daughter learning foreign languages one day. Once she has acquired the first language under very hard circumstances, new next lan-guages will be easy to learn. Since I have been trying to get her to become "fluent" in just more than 30 words, the suggestion about foreign languages sounds like something from another planet. Dr. Traugott clearly sees in her something everyone has missed. She not only sees but makes things happen in front of my eyes right here in her home office in St. Petersburg. She has already become the first person to be able to make my daughter respond to her name. And it took her less than 30 minutes to do so. After everyone else had been trying it for five long years! She clearly knows what she is doing. She understands what my daughter is about.

She talks at a truly professional level with me, the level at which I had been expecting to have discussions with speech therapists, special educators, audiologists – the discussions that never took place and were substituted with accusing me as a "guilty" mother, or her as an "unteachable child" instead. I had not realized that my daughter's issues were beyond the knowledge of every single discipline involved and professional we met. There couldn't have been any explanation/intervention ready to use. Accusing me of being an "incapable" mother by all those specialists seemed to serve as a way to hide their own "incapability" within their profession. A mother of a child cannot be responsible for the lack of knowledge in a scientific field. Feeling the weight of this damaging attitude on my shoulders for so many years has made me question whether non-medical clinicians like speech therapists and special educators may need to consider implementing ethical standards similarly to physicians. Taking the Hippocratic oath pledging to "either help or do no harm" may provide much needed guidance before getting involved in decisions and practices that determine children's participation in society and their quality of life for the rest of their lives.

The way Dr. Traugott makes me feel here in her home in St. Petersburg while we discuss the brain, language, and development during the following week is a new experience in my life as a mother of my troubled child. She is leading thorough discussions with me about brain functions, including auditory processing at lower and higher cortical levels. For me, these discussions are not just necessary – these are also enjoyable. We discuss how the brain makes sense of sound patterns and what skills are required to be able to recognize a spoken word. We discuss the role of auditory scene, auditory memory, and auditory attention in spoken language recognition. In addition to her knowledge, experience, and willingness to share this knowledge, she also touches me at the deepest human level. She approaches me with dignity, respect as a human being, and as a person who has given birth to my child – the feeling I don't recall being a part of me for many years. I feel valued. Respected. Encouraged. Safe. Empowered.

Dr. Traugott shows me her book – a monography published in 1975 that covers her work with these children since the 1930s together with S.I. Kaidanova who addressed sensory aspects of aphasia in adults: *Auditory Impairment in Sensory Alalia and Sensory Aphasia*. Dr. Traugott herself came up with the term "sensory alalia" to describe the condition responsible for the lack of speech development in these particular children. "Alalia" (*a*- priv + *lalia*- talking) – meaning that children have failed to develop speech instead of losing it afterwards. In contrast, the term "aphasia" refers to the loss of previously acquired speech. There is a foundational difference between these two conditions of the lack of speech: when a person loses speech after acquiring it, it means that that person has developed previously the ways that led to language development; when a person has never developed language, the underlying processes of language development have been never developed to the extent that makes language acquisition possible. "Sensory" means that the reason behind these children failing to acquire speech is due to the impairment of non-linguistic sensory systems.

Despite the descriptions of children with normal intelligence who don't learn to speak dating back to the nineteenth century, Dr. Traugott and her team developed the understanding further by investigating these children from the auditory system functioning perspective. She had worked together with Orbeli from Pavlov's lab and collaborated with Luria to identify the characteristics that distinguish developmental lack of speech from adult aphasic syndromes. What she found was that the lack of auditory attention to sound field and connecting sounds to meaning was the underlying problem in these children – the particular non-speech auditory impairment that was not seen in children with sensorineural hearing loss. This means that the usual ways of language acquisition – encouraging children to talk via verbal interaction don't work for these children.

Dr. Traugott is convinced that a child's mother has a primary role in rehabilitating and educating such a child. In order to make a substantial change in her development, learning must be carried out in a targeted way throughout the days, must be of interest to her, and should involve as many family members and close relatives as possible. So that she can learn to adapt to different vocal characteristics and ways of communicating of family members who care about her. She has to learn firsthand that a spoken word has the same linguistic meaning whether it is spoken by a male, female, or child in the same context. Dr. Traugott asks also about music in our family. She says that it is very important to stimulate her auditory system with a full range of sound frequencies in the speaking range since our auditory system is tonotopically organized – sounds are spatially arranged both in the inner ear and the auditory brain. The cochlea itself is like a rolled up piano where high frequency sounds stimulate one end, and low frequency sounds another end. Frequencies do matter. Piano is a must in learning to attach sounds to meaning since it enables us to use a wide range of sound frequencies in a natural way. I feel relieved. I have no trouble understanding the connection between the sounds – whether piano, violin, or any other sounds – and how they combine into meaningful patterns. This has been my life in music since I can ever remember. Also, I have no problem with understanding the role of motivation and practice reaching proficiency in anything we do. I have lived it while achieving mastery in both violin and piano playing. So, I don't care how much time and effort it needs to make it work for my daughter. All I think about is that it *can* be done. Deep inside, I feel that this is the beginning of the rest of my life.

I learn that my daughter has to quickly acquire access to language and information, by learning to read by herself. Teaching her to read would be like providing glasses or Braille instruction to individuals with visual impairments. Learning to read by herself will make the world accessible. Since her brain has problems with auditory information – recognizing and extracting important sounds from less important ones so that speech stream can be followed – auditory learning will be always compromised. But her visual system doesn't have those issues – it is working very well. So, the visual system is the one that she can use to quickly and on the go make sense of the world if appropriately stimulated. It would have been most effective to start a couple of years ago, at age three. We have missed a lot of valuable time. But at age five, it would be still possible, Dr. Traugott says. Neuroplasticity is still good at this age. Her visual strengths make reading the quickest pathway to catch up on the information out there in the world that her peers access through conversation. Access to information through reading means accessing and enhancing her thinking processes and memory. It connects her to the world. The development would be different from her peers who first learn language, and then reading, using most likely a phonetic approach, which requires the ability to detect very fast changes in short duration sounds and their patterns. For her, it would be learning to read having only minimal vocabulary, and then learning to speak through reading, using a whole word approach. Learning through phonetics would never work for her.

I am aware of the widespread belief among educators that learning to read using a phonetic approach is the only effective way. I am wondering whether the professionals who advocate against the whole word approach to reading realize that this may be the only option for many children to access communication via language and participation in the society. When the auditory system is compromised, the visual approach to read enables access to the information in the world – spoken language is compromised anyway. For these children, including my daughter, only whole word recognition as an image, a picture may be possible, providing a way to learn also to speak. So she can learn to articulate the words she reads, not the other way around.

We discuss the importance of math. Math is critical for her intellectual development since it provides a medium to explore reasoning and problem solving endlessly without a need for linguistic proficiency. Therefore, math skills should be developed apart from language. Math is a symbolic system itself. It takes time to learn language, so relying on learning math through language means that she will be always not just delayed in math, but would miss a unique opportunity to connect to the world through exploring and discovering number relationships, their patterns, and schemas. But she shouldn't be. Dr. Traugott shows me a simple way to get started – how to learn the numbers using problem solving instead of counting. She advises against the common practice of counting to avoid supporting the automatic behavior she has been showing for years.

We talk about conditioning. Classic conditioning and operant conditioning. During the following week she continues to teach me about what is known about language organization in the brain, and how this knowledge can be used to develop my daughter. I learn from Dr. Traugott. I spend all the days during the following week with Dr. Traugott. Discussion after discussion. About language and brain. Neuropsychology of language. About conditioning. About what makes us human. I am glad that I decided to study medicine after 15 years of intensive music education. I am glad that I already have several years of experience with neurological patients – stroke, brain tumors, aphasia. I am glad that when I was growing up, our family dinner talk involved topics like topical diagnostics of neurological conditions. My father, highly skilled in neurology, used to give me an exercise after exercise to figure out the location of a lesion in the brain according to the symptoms of patients. Without the ability to think medically, particularly in the field of neurology, I would have trouble understanding fully the thinking behind what Dr. Traugott is saying.

Meeting with a special educator and speech pathologist specializing in minimally verbal children: more than just a teaching program

Dr. Traugott arranges for us to meet with a longtime colleague of hers – a special educator and speech pathologist, Mrs. Golovina. She is about to show me and my daughter how the current knowledge of language organization in the brain can be used in practice. She has been with Dr. Traugott for decades and is already retired, but agrees to see us in her home.

When we enter her apartment, my expectation is that she is just going to talk to me and, provide a layout of a program and show me how to work with my daughter. We are in a foreign country, seeing a foreign speech pathologist/special educator who is a specialist in her own native language, not ours. I expect to learn from her how she does it in her language, and then translate it into our language. I don't expect her to work with my daughter in person. Moreover, my daughter has never sat down at the table and worked with anybody together at all.

I am wrong. Mrs. Golovina is very much interested in connecting with my daughter. As it appears, she has been working with children from many different countries and languages. Initiating the basic human verbal communication and literacy learning is what she has been doing – it's so similar across the cultures. She seems very warm, active, outgoing, relating, and powerful. I don't think that anyone we have met professionally before has displayed these qualities simultaneously. Particularly the combination of powerful and warm. The "powerful" has been connected always to something negative, whether predicting that she would never talk, read etc., or accusations that I as a mother am the reason why she does not speak and behave. But "powerful" as a way to invite my daughter to join in, to connect with her in order to establish a relationship that enables her to teach her, has not been our experience. Mrs. Golovina seems to have a specific body language and presence – the qualities that we have not seen in any speech and language specialists, educators, or medical professionals we have met before. She looks like she has a "stage presence" of a performer who fills the whole stage and commands the full attention from an audience to connect with her.

To my surprise, when Mrs. Golovina asks my daughter – by gesturing and verbalizing it in her native language – to take a seat at the table, she does it. I can't believe my eyes! She is sitting at the table and looking at Mrs. Golovina, like she is waiting for the next order to be given! How is this happening? We are in a new environment – another country, culture, language. Anybody who knows my daughter would think that an unknown environment would not work for her. Anyone would expect the opposite as a result of being in unfamiliar surroundings. Contrary to these expectations, the atmosphere for learning has been somehow already created before the actual work with visual and auditory aspects of words even begin. Did the first ever response to her name two days ago make a difference to how she relates to others now? How is this all possible? As stunned as I was just two days ago watching her respond to her name for the first time ever – when Dr. Traugott was calling her from various distances using various loudness levels while doing so – I am now watching her looking into Mrs. Golovina's eyes and waiting for what she is about to do next with her. Looking into the eyes of another person? Waiting for another person to give a sign for something? How does Mrs. Golovina have so much power on her? What have I and everybody else been missing while trying to connect with her that Mrs. Golovina has? Is it just her personality, or has she learned it from those children whom she has helped to turn verbal and literate? Could it be the basic quality necessary to succeed with her teaching system? Effective reciprocal nonverbal engagement before learning to read and verbalize one's own thoughts and feelings?

The ultimate goal is to provide her with tools so she can learn to read as fast as possible so that language can start developing. How? Until now, my daughter has been playing by herself – developing herself through constructing Lego buildings and putting complicated picture and 3D puzzles together. Now she is expected to do something *with* someone she has never met before. How will Mrs. Golovina make her interested in learning to read? She has shown no interest in looking at the pictures in a children's picture book as speech therapists had recommended before. How is she supposed to learn to read without looking into a book together with someone? She has never agreed to sit down and do something *together*. I don't know how this is going to work. But here we are. Mrs. Golovina is determined to work with her. I am about to learn how to start with reading, vocabulary, speaking, auditory development, math when there is no language other than 30 words and the only processes to base it on would be the capacity for basic comparison and categorization.

Mrs. Golovina's approach proves to be nothing that had been recommended by speech therapists before that hadn't got us anywhere. Differently from other speech therapists whose methods didn't work for years, Mrs. Golovina doesn't ask my daughter to look at the pictures together with her, talk about them, or read together with her. Instead, Mrs. Golovina takes a role of a person who *provides* my daughter with puzzles to solve and then *shares* her happiness in a highly emotional way when done correctly. These are not picture puzzles that require my daughter to recognize which piece goes where so that the whole can be constructed, but reading instruction presented in a way that requires my daughter to respond similarly to puzzle solving. My daughter's role is not to just follow Mrs. Golovina, but solve the exercises as puzzles that are specifically designed to teach her to read under the circumstances when there is no language. This approach requires my daughter to become engaged in the activities requiring the similar skills she has been so good at when building Legos or solving puzzles, Mrs. Golovina's puzzles are just different types of puzzles that address the foundation of any language learning – comparison, categorization, patterns, blending. The idea is to communicate clearly to her the differences between contrasting objects like toys, and contrasting corresponding words that she can look at as pictures. That two objects look different and the spoken words symbolizing the very same objects sound different. And that the written words look different. All at the same time.

Mrs. Golovina explains that the learning materials have to be presented in a way that she can approach these as active problem-solving exercises instead of passive labeling of objects. She wants her to connect her thinking to what she sees and experiences during these early stages of learning. So that she can learn a concept of language through learning to differentiate, categorize, finding patterns, blending. Without the ability to categorize and contrast, language cannot develop. Mrs. Golovina keeps emphasizing the role of presenting learning materials in a highly contrasting manner, so that comparison and categorization, the integral parts of symbolic thinking leading to language acquisition, can be employed immediately. Her main focus is engaging her not just in joint attention and joint action, but in joint thinking. I am learning how conditioning looks in language learning at the most basic level. From object to meaning. And fading of the conditioning. Auditory development to detect spoken words, and then phrases. However, I can't help but notice that getting my daughter engaged in her proposed activities started before the activities began, before any reward was given to her. Apparently, she did not actually join in the activities because of a piece of candy for her good work, but before that. The engagement seems to be a result of other factors than just a piece of candy or other reward.

It feels surreal to be seen by a foreign special educator and speech pathologist for my child's problems. The truth is, at this basic level of language acquisition it is all similar. All across the cultures. Just different vocabulary. However, I realize that the extraordinary way Mrs. Golovina has been interacting with my daughter may form a vital prerequisite that makes teaching a child like her possible. My first impression is that Mrs. Golovina is like a performer on a stage who knows how to get an audience to join in with clapping to the music she creates live. She certainly has succeeded with my daughter against all odds. I take a serious notice.

Back home

We begin. From the beginning. Systematically. Just me and her. I quit my job as a medical doctor so I can be a full-time mother, teacher, and therapist. Being responsible both for my patients' lives and my daughter's development without any professional help from speech therapists, special educators, and without emotional support from people around me leaves me without any other option. My husband seems to have nothing against this arrangement, although he is not willing to offer any support other than financial. Pressured by his family, he had already given up on her. However, his parents are in shock when they learn that I have taken time off from my professional life and am not contributing to the household. His mother sees my devotion to our daughter's development without working my "day job" as a medical doctor as unfair to her son and becomes very vocal about it. According to my mother-in-law, my daughter and I, who had already ruined her son's life, are adding just another tragedy – no salary from me. But I have new hope and I am willing to do whatever I can for my daughter. It's so simple for me.

Why existing learning materials don't allow me to communicate the contrasts that lead to comparison and categorization – the basic components of symbolic language

I am looking for appropriate vocabulary cards. Where objects are shown in the most basic way, without additional information, only a clear singular meaning. I look everywhere I can think of. General education, special education, toy stores, book stores. Very soon I come to the conclusion that they don't exist. All educational materials come highly illustrated. They are not designed for children like her. The simplest vocabulary cards display both a picture and a word together on a card, so that words cannot be mixed, and matched to the picture. Also, the pictures are too colorful. Or the words are presented by syllables, the phonetic approach. Since the problem is in attaching meaning to objects and sound patterns, syllables and phonemes do not have the power that whole words have – the meaning. They are not whole. They can change the meaning, but they don't represent meaning by themselves. She needs whole words. She needs choices. She needs thinking. Matching. Associating. Categorizing. Most educational materials have too many colors, too many different objects, shapes. Too much information. Which meaning can be communicated when there are so many of these in one single picture?

The only way to proceed is to make the vocabulary cards myself. The most basic images of objects, by categories. Animals, Fruits and vegetables, House, Traffic, Family. Separate word cards for each object, one set written in different colors, and another set in a single black color. So they can be mixed up, paired, sorted into different categories based on meaning, the length of a spoken word, color of a word card. Used simultaneously in a variety of ways while communicating a singular meaning. Just like spoken language. The same word said by different people is still the same word, even though it comes in a variety of ways.

I plan to start with the category "Animals." Picture cards. Word cards. Toys. I choose two simple picture cards of two very differently shaped animals, one represented by a single syllable word and the other by a three-syllable word. I choose the toys and images of "bird" and "elephant" as a starting point because these creatures *look* very different; the words representing them *sound* very different; images of written words representing these animals look also very different; when the actual toys are touched, they *feel* very different. There is no language I can use to explain anything. The communication can begin only by looking, hearing, touching. Whatever aspect of the image or toy she may choose, whether visual, auditory or tactile. This highly contrasting pair of objects of the same category seems to be relevant in this situation. An elephant has a unique body design that makes it hard to confuse with any other animal in the world: a long trunk, tusks, large flappy ears, four strong legs. A bird has none of these characteristics. Very different visual characteristics.

Also, very different acoustic characteristics. A three-syllable word vs. a one-syllable word. A different number of syllables means a different structure when spoken. Also, a sharply different duration of the spoken words representing these objects: long vs. short; contrasting rhythmic patterns of "ti-ti-ta" vs. "ta-a"; a melodic contour of descending direction for "elephant" vs. a more constant level for "bird"; different pitches due to different speech sounds for both words.

Moreover, written words for these images look different: a long word vs. a short written word; different letters composing these particular two words in a written form. When she notices just one letter in a written word, she can tell these words apart already. Sharp contrasts in multiple ways: visual, auditory, touch. The main idea is to try to communicate that these two objects are different, and that they can be recognized by comparing their contrasting characteristics by looking, hearing, and/or touching.

Words are written in different colors. 'Bird' in red color and 'Elephant' in blue. Without reading, it can be looked at just as one red smaller image consisting of some elements, and a blue larger image consisting of more elements. Contrast is what I am trying to communicate first. Fewer letters in a small red picture and more letters in a larger blue picture. No attempts for syllabic division, no phonetic approach. Just a word as a picture. A whole. With a meaning. She can use a color to associate a word card to the corresponding image. She can just detect that the red word goes with a bird picture, and the blue word with an elephant picture. I prepare small pieces of candy. Any act of interaction towards the goal will be worthy of rewarding. So she can build a sense of self, satisfaction, and pride.

In earlier years, she articulated many words, even seemed to know their meaning for a short duration, and then they all disappeared, without proceeding into phrases and sentences – into language. It was not enough to know a word. A word without thinking involved may mean nothing more than just a vibration in the air.

The question still is how to get her to sit at a table similarly to Mrs. Golovina, and how to develop sustained attention, focus. How to make her interested in learning? How to create a joint attention with joint action? How to begin? It's not just making her learn. It is creating a trusting first ever relationship while introducing her to learning. It is about creating the environment where synchronization of feelings and actions – hers and mine – can take place, and reciprocity develop. Although, I witnessed just a week ago how Mrs. Golovina's powerful presence made a difference that no one else has ever achieved – a moment to moment communication between two people where words don't matter so much, if at all.

Building meaningful interaction at a glance: the importance of speed

We start in the living room. I want her to sit down at the coffee table so we can work on building the vocabulary. Although it may seem that nothing is happening yet, the atmosphere is intense. The way I approach her, trying to catch her attention, and make her respond by following my directions to sit down. She would not respond to words that seem to mean nothing to her. She would not respond to my peaceful gestures either. Without standing out from the general environment, the gestures would remain unnoticeable, or without any significance for her. Or she would not understand that these mean a request, or a suggestion, and that she is expected to respond, whether by denying or following. It would be so easy to try to connect with her in any way possible, and still not end up with anything significant that can be considered a response. To communicate, a highly intensified approach seems to be necessary. So, I have to make my request bold enough to be noticed by her, and bold enough to be perceived as a request, instead of a label or statement without a communicative value. If I just talked and gestured without boldness, speed and intensity, she would not notice in a way that requires a response, a communicative action from her. And if I succeeded with getting her attention, and then just talked, she would not understand what I am saying, and would be not be interested in it. Getting her attention would be the first important step, but it has to be followed fast and actively by inviting her into action. This is how it feels to me when my goal is just to get her to sit down, so we could start working on the vocabulary.

Instead of using words, that have failed to build communication with her for five and a half years, I am using movement to convey my message. Without fast action, I cannot stand out from the general environment – so, I use speed. I move quickly into her view. And then quickly communicate what I want by further movement towards the table. And then make her follow. No more than 5 seconds altogether. The changing direction of my body, first towards her, and then towards the table. The dynamics of movement, the change in speed, from short high-intensity initial movement, followed by a short pause lasting about 1–2 seconds, before switching into inviting her to follow the request. Like a three-step interaction: (1) get her attention; (2) direct her attention to the chair at the table; (3) ignite movement in her. Quick, clear, and with purpose. With a beginning, central part, and an end. A message, a story, a request told in movement.

The way I approach her is intense. The intensity is not much different from when I play a simple phrase with a violin. Both with clear and sharp beginning, building intensity, developing it further, and taking it to resolve. However, both playing solo or playing with other musicians, music doesn't start with the first note but before any sound is played. It starts with communicating the intention to start at a certain fraction of a second. It involves body movement, gestures, timed to communicate the exact beginning, mood, even rhythm. During this preparatory phase of music making, there is no music to help to communicate, it's all about communication *without* sound, when everyone adjusts their motor planning to be able to synchronize the exact timing of sound events. I decide to use this type of nonverbal communication consisting of carefully timed sequence of gestures and body movements in 3D space to hopefully engage my daughter in joint action.

My intensive music training that started during the first years of my life becomes handy. I grew up as being part of the music and learned to read music before reading books. This is a way I know, and which is so natural to me. I don't have to think about it. I have it ready in my mind and body, and I go for it. Ready to act in a split second. Ready to immediately develop it further. Ready to turn everything else off in my mind to be fully present. Ready to interact. Ready to build. Ready to adjust. I realize that my medical thinking is not enough to create action with her. I need my extensive music making experience now. I even need my experience as a performing non-classical music artist that involves playing music for large audiences where creating a contact with an audience is a skill itself.

The combination of both – music and medicine – is what enables me to translate knowledge into action now and hopefully create a relationship with my daughter while taking together her first steps in literacy learning. I had not realized the importance of this nonverbal engagement before I saw it in action when we were visiting Mrs. Golovina for her special education and speech pathology advice.

When I approach my daughter, my communication is sincere, without any other thoughts or feelings separating us. I don't think about the future, how she is going or not going to develop, how is she going to be as an adult. I don't think what has gone wrong that we have this current situation. I don't think what if she doesn't respond. My communicative attempt with her doesn't include any doubts. The only thing that matters is the current moment and to make the most out of it. Like playing my violin. When my bow gets into contact with a string, nothing else matters. It is only about making the most of it.

A thought can be communicated and expressed in movement with similar intensity, structure, and timeframe as it would be in spoken language or music making. When I approach her to get her attention, I obstruct her view with a fast and intense movement. She slows for a second whatever she is doing. This becomes the first synchronized connection with her. I respond with a pause in my movement. When I continued without a short 1–2 second lasting pause, I would not give her an opportunity to respond. Her slowing down would get lost and would not enable her to direct her attention to the chair and respond with her body following my body direction and gestures. Like a pause in music, a moment of silence that prepares for the next, that very likely something else, even more important is coming. When the pause is too long, it would lose its power for an expectation for something to happen. So naturally, it lasts about 1–2 seconds, when we experience this first connection – her slowing down, and me pausing immediately in response to her slowing down. And then as a new wave, I initiate a new movement with increments of increasing intensity, inviting her to join me: I change in a fluid manner my body direction towards the table and chair while showing with my hand gesture to take her seat. Again, my movement can be looked more like a poetic or musical phrase than just changing my location. It could be regarded as an invitation to accompany my violin playing with her own instrument. To join in, to provide something by herself, but in synchronization with me. So that harmony can be created. I provide the frame and she fills in.

After the initial slowing down, she does follow me with her body, ending up sitting down at the table, her attention still turned on, ready for something else to come. The next pause cannot last more than a couple of seconds, or it will lose its power to serve as an expectation for something to happen again. She is sitting now and I have to be immediately ready to provide the new setting, so that the "next" can happen. Within a couple of seconds.

Bringing life into vocabulary cards

The picture cards and written word cards are not interesting when they are lying still on the table, ready to be looked at. They may easily mean nothing. There is no action. Nothing to follow with her eyes. No reason to pay attention – picture and written word cards lying on the table would not go anywhere. To get her attention and interest in these cards, action has to be created. With the speed of approximately one card per second or matching the heartbeat, I am placing these cards by one on the table in front of her: (1) the first picture card; (2) the second picture card; (3) the first written card matching the first picture; (4) the second written word card matching the second picture. Followed by a 1–2 second pause. She is following with her eyes my demonstration, each card from 1 to 4. Her eyes go to the left and right, up and down. She is not looking at me, but she is looking at the cards. I don't know what she is thinking, or what is she even noticing about these. She seems interested and alert. During the next 1–2 second pause she has a chance to have extra time to look before I quickly pick all the cards up. The table becomes empty again. Everything gone. Like in speech or music: a phrase or sentence is gone after it is said or played on an instrument. What is left, is memory. Does she have something about these cards in the memory now? I don't know until I give her the next chance.

In order to keep her attention and her expectation up for something to happen next, I place the two picture cards back on the table, but hand over the written word cards to her. She responds by taking these into her hands. I use a small hand gesture towards the picture cards on the table, trying to encourage her to match these, but it seems unnecessary. She is already placing the written word cards next to the corresponding picture cards. All correctly and fast. She did store the combinations in her memory from my demonstration! I respond to her achievement with high praise, jumping up from my chair, showing my happiness and satisfaction with my facial expressions, body expressions, movement, and verbal praise with highly emotional voice. Like her achievement is the highest in the world. Her eyes meet my eyes for a short moment and she shows a smile on her face, not matching my intensity, but certainly matching the timing. My first true communication with her has become alive and meaningful. It is all about the present moment. Nothing matters from the past and the future is unknown anyway. But the roadmap has been created.

Since she had just been able to respond, focus, and act purposefully, I question whether I should increase the number of objects immediately to keep up her interest with optimal stimulation in relation to her true abilities, the extent of which is unknown for me at this time. This thought is my split-second reaction to her successful performance, occurring immediately after we finish our approximately 3-second shared celebration of her success with the first set. Now, during the next short 2–3 second pause (5 second interruption of interaction would be too long to keep her attention alive), I am not only recognizing my thought, but turning it into a quick decision and action. The decision I have to make in a fraction of a second now is about whether to proceed with two new picture/word cards only, or to combine these with the two from the previous activity and increase the number of objects to work on immediately to four. I'll go with just two new picture cards and corresponding written word cards, afraid of increasing the number too fast. I quickly grab two additional picture cards and two word cards to work on.

During these critical first moments of creating true interaction, synchronization being an integral part of it, my own feelings have gone through the following sequence: from tension while inviting her to join in with me without knowing beforehand whether she reciprocates, to wonder and curiosity whether she recognized and memorized the relationships between picture and written word cards; to pleasant surprise when she immediately steps into action, to satisfaction when she matches the cards correctly; to joy when meeting her eyes with my eyes and exchange a smile during our shared celebration; to fear that I am not stimulating her according to her unknown abilities, both too much and too little stimulation and not being able to keep up the speed so she would not lose connection with me. Like a rollercoaster ride with high speed and unpredictability, but during which quick decisions and actions have to be made. For me, it feels like playing the Wieniawski violin concerto in D minor, particularly its third movement (Allegro con fuoco – "with great vigor and speed") with high speed, feeling of fire, technical virtuosity, and rapid and unexpected emotional fluctuations. The same concerto that I had graduated with from the music school just before my medical studies. The only difference is that in the violin concerto, the score has been created, the combinations of its components – notes, their pitch, duration, patterns were predetermined by the composer Henri Wieniawski. In this situation, I have to create both the "score" and the "music" of the interaction myself, a lot of it "on the go," while matching the general aspects of playing the concerto – speed, feeling of fire, intensity, technicality, and emotionality. I am creating two parts simultaneously to be acted out – one for me and one for her. I initiate, provide a frame and invite her to join in to play her part. Like a performer igniting interest in the audience and asking in nonverbal ways the audience to join in by clapping in the rhythm of music. And when she responds, I listen, adjust and create my response. And then initiate again, depending on her response. Continuously. Making sure that emotions are actually communicated, not only "notes" or "words" and their patterns. While she is keeping her attention, it's harmony with urgency, controlled internal fire, followed by an unexpected romance, then urgency again, followed by a complex but beautiful celebration, coming out of nowhere but bringing the feeling of relief – all of it synchronized in the frame of a steady beat, never giving up, never stopping more than to breathe before the next phrase. I have to keep it up and going, or we will be lost and need to start over again. All of it may seem like working just on the vocabulary, unless one can look deeper and see what is happening "backstage."

I find myself taking my own first steps in learning something new while exploring the area of creating a human relationship from scratch. A world I did not know anything about before. However, through my personal experience in performing music with various groups and in a variety of settings, I have been highly aware of the special relationships between the musicians as they perform, but not outside the music medium. I am excited to discover this parallel world of people relating to each other without playing music together, along with my involvement with my own child's wellbeing. I realize that while she is becoming more aware of her surroundings, I must allow myself to become the enabler of her success and development. I realize that it is up to me to allow both of us to build trust and will, instead of blocking it with ready-made judgements, assumptions, and fears. I feel that at this point, it is up to me to allow her to discover words in relation to objects, instead of just me or anybody else trying to teach those to her. That it is up to me to allow her to form her own experience under my guidance, and develop a human relationship instead of trying to teach social and other skills to her. And that it is up to me to allow her to recognize her own feelings through her own explorations, feedback, and trial and error, instead of trying to teach her to recognize facial expressions, or attempting to make her life just happy. It is not just her who is learning, it's also me. The relationship we are trying to establish and strengthen doesn't work when it's one-sided. I have to continuously adjust how I relate to her to match it with her development. It feels like I allow myself to become not just a partner sharing her experiences, but an upgraded partner for every new step she is taking on the trajectory of development under my guidance. I have to allow myself to change in a way. Creating "music" together while continuously matching continuously developing "musicians' skills" – this is what life seems to be about.

Month No. 1, January 1992

Discovering the first critical hour each and every day

The critical time leading or not leading to a successful day appears to be the beginning of these carefully preplanned activities. Every morning is truly a new beginning. This is a time when the relationship has to be reestablished, and a switch to focus and attention to our joint activities recreated. It is not about remembering the words or activities from the previous day. It is all about recreating the same relationship that we created a day before, but which seemed to disappear overnight.

I realize very soon that the key to initiating an increasingly longer-lasting connection is the timing of the initial communication attempts and pauses in between these. When you press a single piano key, the sound has a really brief duration, but when you hit the next piano key while the vibrations from the previous sound are still in the air, you create a whole melody that has a meaning. When pressing piano keys too infrequently, they remain just single sounds without a true connection. Or like heart beats with optimal durations and pauses in between. Similarly, when I get her visual attention for a second, I have to immediately invite her into an action that has a meaning for her. And then, before her interest fades, the next visual attention, followed by the next invitation to act. In this way, she becomes a doer – doing, initiating, responding, and taking in.

I learn that she has to be continuously stimulated, or she drops out from our interaction. This means, that I have to be prepared for a high speed inter-action with a variety of opportunities for new appropriate activities ready to be used that build on each other. In order to be able to quickly adapt to her attention and interest, all learning materials have to be prepared, ready to use, and provide a variety to choose from, so I can respond appropriately in a split second. She cannot wait and keep her interest with doing nothing. No break more than for 5–10 seconds. A 15-second pause and we have to start building attention and interest from the beginning again. There is no time to get something from another room, or prepare something on the go. Actually, I cannot even leave the table without losing the connection with her. The very same connection we had just built together. It seems so fragile.

However, over and over again, I learn that after an hour of keeping this extremely high intensity of interaction up, she begins to do it by herself, but only when work provided for her ignites her interest. I also notice that her appearance changes during this critical hour: she generally becomes more calm and her eyes seem more clear and present. She looks like a different child from the one just an hour ago. I learn the deep impact of this critical first hour of continuous intensity that seems to change her at some very deep level. During this first hour we become a team. With shared attention. Shared focus. She seems to get ready for learning. After this first hour, she starts to do and demand interaction by herself. She seems to get satisfaction out of her achievement of figuring out which cards and toys go where. She demands it. Asks using a very clear word "more." Clearly, she feels good. Organized. Relief from something that she had before but has been cleared out of the way now. Surprisingly, she starts to demand learning activities from me for the next several hours in a row – the duration of attention and focusing I could never even imagine to be possible for her outside of lining up objects in circles and other shapes. I also realize that any evaluations during the first hour of interaction would be dramatically different from those carried out now, an hour later after an intense warm-up.

Month No. 2, February 1992

She can easily recognize an object just by looking at the written word and find that object – a picture or a toy in a room. It's much harder to listen to a word I say and then find an appropriate written word card, toy or picture. I follow the guidelines of Mrs. Golovina and say the words to her under three different conditions: (1) facing her directly so she can use the cues from my mouth movements, facial expressions, and body movements; (2) covering my mouth with a screen so she can use only my general facial and body movements without seeing my lips; (3) standing behind her while saying the words so she cannot see me at all – using only her auditory system without visual help. The latter is the most difficult since she has to detect also *when* a sound – a spoken word – is occurring in a general auditory scene, extract it from other simultaneously occurring environmental sounds like fans and street traffic. Under these three conditions I keep my voice – the pitch, speed, loudness the same for each set of trials. She learns to compare what she hears to what is stored in her memory from previous experience, figure out which object, picture, written word this sound refers to by using a variety of sound characteristics available like the length of the word, the syllabic structure, rhythmic and melodic contour, pitch range. She learns also that sound medium connects her with me whether she can see me or not. My voice, my vocal timbre, my vocal pitch range are the unique characteristics of me in addition to my visual appearance. She learns that she can physically relate to me not only via body movement, gestures, touch – but also via sound alone. She discovers that I can be present even when she doesn't see me.

In order to learn to connect with me purposefully via sound, I encourage her to say the words we are working on after me. She had previously learned to say about 30 words, so she has some experience with vocalizing. Now I am expecting her vocalizations to expand in parallel with visual language learning. At the exact moment when her hand places a written word card on a toy or a picture I encourage her to voice that word. During that split second, I lean in towards her and raise my hand to direct by gesturing to say that word after me. My whole body gets activated to encourage her to say that word: my arms are up and extended, prompting her to initiate her act of speaking while providing a visual expression of the melodic and rhythm contour of that particular spoken word. It becomes like a subsection of our script – we don't proceed without this part happening. The timing of this few seconds every single time seems to help to communicate that her vocal response is required, and that has to happen exactly at that particular time. She can always expect it, so she has to be ready to act on it. Her thinking when making a decision about "which card goes where" is followed by a gross motor action – physically moving the objects, and then adding another, a fine motor action – vocalizing the object in spoken language.

However, repeating a word after me reveals a different set of problems. She seems to do everything not to say any words. It isn't just *not* saying, but actively working against saying. She likes to do visual matching which is great, but without getting her to say the words, she fails to develop spoken language. Candy or whatever she may wish as a prize, seems to be here the most appropriate to use for rewarding. Just praising does not work – she has to really wish to get something in exchange of saying the words, the hardest or unwanted thing for her to do. The way she articulates when interested enough due to gaining a reward seems puzzling – her vocal approximations of words are without any clear phonemes. Like not enough pixels in a picture. I get a feeling that she does not perceive individual speech sounds, but general melodic and rhythmic contours along with the duration of the words. Because this is how her "spoken words" sound. A melodic contour with matched duration and rhythm. Usually high-pitched. And only shadows of phonemes. But I also realize that her muscles have not developed enough to speak clearly and in a timely manner. It makes sense to me – how can the perception of speech sounds and muscle control of speaking muscles develop without being actively involved in speaking?

Remarkably, the number of words she is successfully working on is increasing fast. I rearrange the images/toys/ word cards after each round she completes to increase the difficulty level as immediately as possible. Matching corresponding toys to the pictures and word cards and vice versa. Multiple ways and correlations. Literacy learning simultaneously with the first basic vocabulary learning. For increasingly more hours each day. Alternating with other activities that reinforce the learned words and concepts: music, outside, zoo, food, and toy stores. Very soon, the total length of all the activities, each of them connected to language/literacy learning, will reach 12 hours each day.

Joint attention seems to be developing, occasional brief eye contact may or may not happen, motivation/self-satisfaction of "doing" and "solving" seems to get a real start. Expectation for praise and reward is growing each day. No question, we interact. However, looking more closely, our interaction during matching–saying–reward–expecting is not actually a representative of a conversation with regular back and forth sharing of thoughts and feelings with sustained reciprocal attention. The subject of our interactions are not thoughts and feelings to be shared, but objects to be labeled, categorized, and articulated. The joint attention we develop is about shared objects, and not about sharing thoughts and feelings. It is more like a forced shared experience of vocabulary learning. Not a real conversation.

Taking learning into the Piano Room

Soon I discover, that the way we interact changes dramatically when we take learning into the Piano Room. Here she is free to use any part of the room. We take the same image cards, written word cards, and toys with us. Instead of saying, I play the words on the piano now. Or use a toy to play the word with the piano. My ability of perfect pitch becomes critical here: since I hear music in every word before the linguistic meaning, it is natural for me to just play the music of the words with a musical instrument. For example, the spoken word "elephant" is not just a combination of the speech sounds "\e-l ə -fənt\" but each of these speech sounds has a pitch, a general sound that is shaped into the particular purposeful phonemes. This basic sound is created by the expiration airflow through the larynx that makes vocal communication possible. The pitch of this basic sound allows me to match it with a similar pitch on a piano – a musical instrument with a wide frequency range that covers the pitch ranges of any speaker. This general sound has different acoustic characteristics depending on the speaker – different range for male, female or child speakers, and different pitch intervals depending on the emotional state of a speaker. For example, the stressed syllable of the word "elephant" – a vowel "e" – is usually spoken in a higher pitch than the vowel of the next syllable "\l ə\," the difference may comprise a musical interval of major second, third, fourth or fifth or even larger interval in a "descending" mode, depending on the speaker. Most of the females I know say the word "elephant" when spoken in an indifferent emotional manner using the pitches of D of the first octave (just one step above the middle C) for the first syllable and G of the small octave – an interval of a fifth below the D for the next two syllables while males use the pitches an octave below – D of the small octave for the first syllable and G of the great octave for the next two syllables. When spoken as a surprise, the pitch for the first syllable is usually much higher – even a D of the second octave – while the pitches for the two other syllables are spoken still as G of the small octave – the pitch interval in the emotional state of surprise being much wider – an octave and a fifth instead of just a fifth. When I hear spoken language, I hear those general vocal pitches of the speakers before I recognize the words themselves. I hear the music, my first language, of the spoken words first – the music I can immediately play on a piano.

In addition, my sensitivity to the acoustic properties of sounds allows me to address other acoustic features of the sounds of spoken language in addition to detecting pitches and timbres. It is impossible for me not to notice that speech sounds are spoken with different levels of loudness: the vowel of the stressed syllable "\e\" is spoken louder than the next syllable "\l ə\," and the vowel of the third syllable "\f ənt\" even softer. The loudness contour of the word "elephant" is spoken in a mode of "diminuendo" – a decrease in loudness. Also, the speech sounds of the word "elephant" are vocalized within a conventional timeframe of the general speed of speaking – not too fast or too slow, but just in a tempo that feels right for the conversation. Within the general timeframe, the syllables of the "elephant" are spoken in a certain rhythm – the combined duration of the two first spoken syllables equals to the duration of the third syllable – the rhythm of the word "elephant" sounds "♫ ♩."

In contrast, the word "giraffe" that has different speech sounds "\j ə-'raf\," also has a different pitch contour and intervals of a fourth or fifth between the syllables more likely than any other interval. When the word "elephant" is spoken in a descending pitch mode, then the word "giraffe" is usually spoken in an ascending mode – the first syllable "\j ə\" of "giraffe" is spoken in a lower pitch than the stressed syllable "\raf\." Also, unlike the word "elephant," the dynamic loudness mode for the spoken word "giraffe" is "crescendo" – an increase in loudness – the first syllable being vocalized softer than the second syllable. The rhythm contour is different not only because of the different number of syllables, but also because of the rhythmic pattern of unstressed syllable preceding a stressed one – the duration of the first syllable is a half of that of the second syllable – the rhythm of the word "giraffe" sounds " ♪ ♩ ."

Differently from the words "elephant" and "giraffe," the word "gorilla" is spoken in an ascending pitch mode from the first syllable to the second syllable, and in a descending pitch mode from the second syllable to the third syllable. The loudness contour for the spoken word "gorilla" entails both the "crescendo" and "diminuendo" – an increase in loudness from the first syllable to the second, followed by a decrease in loudness from the second syllable to the third. The rhythm contours of the words "gorilla" and "elephant" differ despite both being three-syllable words. Although the second syllable is stressed in "gorilla," the duration of all three syllables is equal – the rhythm of the word "gorilla" sounds "♪ ♫."

Considering these acoustic patterns, I create the piano versions for spoken words and phrases. This way I can communicate with her directly already – in a way that is related to spoken language use but is not there yet. While still learning just the basic vocabulary, I realize that in a piano room I can create a way for immediate back and forth communication via musical aspects of language – the same vocabulary we learn in another room from the linguistic point of view. I discover that we can share the emotionally communicative content of the spoken words before associating speech sounds with linguistic meaning. When speech sounds of the words are too difficult for her to grasp simultaneously with nonlinguistic acoustic patterns, it may be necessary to start from the acoustic patterns similarly to typically developing infants during the first year of life or even before birth. These acoustic patterns provide a much needed medium for back-and-forth meaningful interaction when language has not developed enough yet. While doing so, I pay extra attention to using the whole frequency range of the piano to communicate that the same pitch, loudness, and rhythm patterns are associated with the same words despite different frequency ranges – similarly to different speakers.

Having the advantage of perfect pitch and having grown up with music from very early childhood, it is easy for me to create various musical activities to address the early communication on the go if I know what we want to achieve. I combine my perception of acoustic features of sounds and my own understanding of the music and language connection with what I learned from Dr. Traugott about the importance of nonlinguistic auditory development in language acquisition. I make it look like a play that addresses acoustic problem solving, and involves visual, auditory, proprioceptive and motor learning simultaneously. Whatever we do in the Piano Room, it looks like a natural and spontaneous play.

Having fun in the Piano Room

I use a paw of the toy dog to play a single sound for the word "dog" – matching the syllabic rhythm. I use a toy gorilla to play three consecutive sounds to match the syllabic rhythm for "gorilla." "Dog" music in medium fundamental frequency range, "gorilla" music in low. She is next to me and is following my playing with her eyes. After this short demonstration, I place the toy animals into the basket. Now I play a similar short music expression for "gorilla." I ask her, by demonstration and gesturing, to find the appropriate toy and put it on the piano. She does it immediately. The same for "dog" music. And other music we create. Simple short improvisations with syllabic rhythm, matching melodic contours, or both. Frequency contrasts. Rhythm contrasts. Duration contrasts. Intensity contrasts. Movements matching music and syllabic rhythm. Every word that we had been working on at the table in the living room is now paired with a short musical expression in the Piano Room. I play a word and she responds by finding a toy or a written word card and places it to a different location – into the basket. It is so easy compared to the setting we use sitting opposite each other in the living room. The Piano Room is full of action. Now it is her turn. She plays a word for this toy now herself – syllabic rhythm. Using any piano keys. She learns to press piano keys, one note per each syllable while saying the words. It does not matter which key. It is only important that she uses her fingers and arm to press the keys. And she attempts to play the rhythm of a word representing a toy on the piano. Duration. Rhythmic pattern. Melodic pattern is what just happens here – improvised by her this time. She discovers different pitches – high and low. She can choose whichever piano keys with different pitches she likes. She is creating sound patterns for these vocabulary words now by herself. I am a listener this time. I respond to her playing and myself place an appropriate toy back into the basket. Sometimes I make intentional "mistakes" – she reacts to these by choosing herself a correct toy.

It seems so much easier to articulate the same words while playing them simultaneously on the piano. The words become alive. More meaningful. Dynamic. It seems there is so much more to a word than just a matching object – a way, a process, a sound pattern, a feeling when we hear it, and a feeling when we respond to it. I learn that her attention is immediately available in the Piano Room, it lasts a long time and does not require an intense warm-up. It makes sense to start the day in the Piano Room and not the other way around.

Music can represent anything we choose to. Vocabulary learning becomes multidimensional with endless possibilities to create a variety of sounds in addition to just saying the words. We create new associations over and over again while keeping the syllabic rhythm the same. It may sound different each time, but the rhythm contour remains. Like in spoken language, where the words have still the same linguistic meaning regardless of whether they are spoken by males, females, children, native or non-native speakers with various accents. The short improvisations become symbols for objects, words, movements. Right there, during the live improvisation. When she does not understand a linguistic or phonemic point I am trying to make, I emphasize in live improvisation that particular music component. I play that part of the word louder, in different frequencies or accents. Since she has shown that she has a problem with following the spoken word from the beginning to the end, matching words with elements of music enables the communication of the full duration of the word – that the word has a beginning, middle, and end. Each part of a word played with different pitches, loudness, timbre.

She reacts and responds to my emphasized version of a musical message without any hesitation or problem.

On the go, we create a special language for our interaction over and over again, where musical aspects of spoken words are emphasized and separated from the actual phonemes of the words. This musical version of words of basic vocabulary becomes an easy and enjoyable way to have a two-way conversation – a back and forth interaction, where music of words is created with piano instead of vocal tract. And then played on a piano while vocalizing simultaneously – each syllable corresponding to a note on a piano. Unexpectedly easy. Flowing. With surprises. It feels like freedom, a relief. Adding music to word learning adds endless possibilities to multiple aspects of literacy. No extra rewards needed here. No behavior modification necessary. Like in usual communication. Freedom and spontaneity. And fun.

Improving the articulation is another aspect of spoken language we address with music. Listening to her puzzling "word approximations" that do include melodic and rhythmic contour of the corresponding word, but no clear phonemes, makes me realize that she actually cannot pronounce words clearly since she has not spoken for five and a half years like other children. Vocal tract needs exercising. Motor control. Both for vowels and consonants, in a variety of combinations. High speed and precise timing.

We expand our musical interaction and add vocal exercises. Like opera singers and choral singers – who need to improve articulation. The same purpose. Making all kinds of combinations of phonemes audible to gain control over the vocal tract. All in music. With various rhythmic patterns to practice speed and timing – both necessary for effective speech production. Using different pitch patterns all across the vocal range to provide a high variety into the activity and into her vocalizations which have been mostly high pitched so far. Vocalizing loud and soft – the variety in loudness perception. I use Kodály early childhood music education principles wherever I can. To explore the duration of sounds, I assign syllables with different lengths to music note patterns. Keeping the beat while vocalizing: normal speed (similar to walking) "TA-TA-TA" vs. quick (similar to running) ti-ti-ti-ti-ti-ti or quick pe-pa-pe-pa-pe vs. elongated vocals E-E-A-A-E-E. Each exercise I accompany with harmonic chords on the piano. It does not matter whether she sounds more like she is singing or more like she is speaking. It is important that she is producing it, and doing it with speed and accuracy, and in a timely manner. She learns to synchronize her vocalization with my chord playing: timing the beginning the syllable pattern, and timing the end of it with rhythmically matched harmonic chords, followed by a deep breath in to prepare for the next pattern in a set. In order to keep up the tempo and vocalize in synchrony, she has to have a visual contact, and a shared feeling of the beat with me. In addition to my hands on the piano keys communicating the exact time to begin her vocalization, I use my head by nodding and body by leaning in to emphasize nonverbally that I am inviting her to join in in that particular fraction of a second. Then we take a deep breath together, synchronized with my hands rising and descending accordingly above the piano keys. She gets the message. After each short pattern, I change the musical key a half step/semitone higher – going through 12 times total using 12 different pitch ranges each time while the rhythm and syllables remain the same. After we have reached an octave higher than we started, I change the musical key to a half step/semitone lower for each repetition. I don't stop in between. It's like a train she has to catch to get on and then keep going while keeping the beat and being ready to voice syllables in time to remain in synchrony with my playing. In total, each syllabic pattern gets voiced musically 24 times in 12 different pitch ranges in less than 1.5 minute. This is approximately up to 200 switches from one syllable to another during this period of time. We usually practice four to five different syllabic patterns in a row that makes the total time for each practice session about 5–7 minutes. During these 5–7 minutes she is continuously playing her part in our jointly created music by articulating different syllables in a synchronized way. She is vocalizing a total of up to 1000 syllables using different pitches and rhythmic patterns during this relatively short time period. This is how including music in a targeted way helps to bring speed, intensity, variety into learning. It provides a component of novelty and freshness while building the capacity for expectation and motor planning. It adds an emotional component necessary to keep her interest up and sustain joint attention. It provides a temporal frame without which the meaningless spoken syllables she needs to practice wouldn't make sense. Spoken syllables become music where she has an opportunity to use her vocal timbre of spoken syllables to connect with the melody and harmony provided by me – all framed in a rhythmic structure. Sometimes I use Kodály hand signs that help to show visually a particular tonal function to emphasize sound relationships via audio–motor–visual system activation. It is amazing to see how her articulation improves during these exercises so fast, which seems to prove that the underuse of the vocal tract had been the underlying issue in motor speech difficulties.

Working in this manner day by day, her meaningful vocabulary, categorization skills – by images, written words, spoken words, sound features like timbre, frequency, rhythmic and melodic patterns, and her capacity for working memory develop with unexpected intensity. Also, fluency in interaction and self-expression.

Taking interaction to public places

Each day we spend an hour or two outside in public spaces to practice interaction in public. Everything is different outside: the attention, connection, interaction, saying just any word at all. It feels like starting from the beginning again every single day regardless of what we had just been achieving inside. The basic connection is different. Talking is hard. Getting her to say anything in public. For example, in a café where I expect her to put her skills to work and ask for her favorite food, it does not happen. Despite knowing that she knows how to ask. And that she desires that particular food so much. I step in an order food for her. Not her favorite, but something else. What happens next is a surprise: she screams "NO" and orders for herself.

Month No. 3, March 1992

Expanding vocabulary to word combinations

We have been working systematically with single vocabulary words from numerous categories in numerous environments for a couple of months now – in a way that requires thinking in order to act. She knows the words, matches without any effort pictures to toys and written word cards up to at least a selection of 12 at a time. Categorizes the words correctly without any effort into appropriate categories: animals, fruits, vegetables, furniture, people, vehicles, colors, etc. Articulates the same words not perfectly but understandably.

We have started to expand the language from single words to two-word, then three-word combinations: when she says "ball, I say "big ball," show a big ball and encourage her to repeat after me. And then the same for "small ball." When she says "big ball," I add immediately "big red ball," or "big blue ball," etc. Toys, picture cards and particularly written word cards get rearranged and combined in multiple ways. Working both at the table in the living room, and at the piano in the Piano Room.

When previously, by creating a system to differentiate each number of syllables on a musical scale, the number of syllables of a word determined how many notes I played altogether for that particular word. Now I play the rhythm, accents, and phrase structure by expanding also the musical representations of single words into musical representations of word combinations. I realize that I need to come up with a composing algorithm, a system that enables me to quickly create musical versions of words that can be combined to form a phrase or a sentence in a meaningful way in a music medium. I develop an approach that enables the creation of a lexicon of musical versions of the words on the go where the first musical note on the scale is determined by the number of syllables but where the next notes can be any combination of the sounds all across the pitch range of an instrument used. This system gives enough structure to the music we create but doesn't limit the use of music into predetermined sound combinations. The syllabic rhythm of a word serves as an ironclad way to connect the music with a word. This dynamic approach gives an opportunity to mix and match the pitch ranges of a musical instrument with corresponding pitch ranges of different speakers, particularly when used with an acoustic piano with wide pitch range corresponding to the acoustic range of human speech. Also, this approach allows me to be creative in adding contrasts as needed to emphasize particular grammar points if necessary.

For example, the word combination "big red ball," which consists of three different one-syllable words would be played in a following way: a single note played a musical interval of an octave higher for "big," and a single note an octave lower for a "red" from a piano key (also a single note), representing a one-syllable noun "ball" in the middle. For "big yellow ball" it would be a single note an octave higher for "big" and two notes a second higher for two-syllable "yellow" from a single note representation for the one-syllable noun "ball." A combination of words in conjunction with a combination of notes. A combination of syllabic rhythms paralleled with a combination of musical rhythms. A combination of word pitch contours paralleled with a combination of musical melodies. A system is born to match the changes in language structure with corresponding changes in music structure. A flexibility of expression rooted in basic structural principles.

Expanding both word combinations and musical note combinations simultaneously not only makes the learning fun and highly interactive, but helps to communicate the system of how language is structured. She likes "expanding" and responds without any significant difficulties. She seems to get relief from something while figuring out relationships between objects themselves, sound patterns related to objects, between language components, and how these can be expressed in music. Also, I have been encouraging her to figure out math in addition to language. Being afraid of supporting automatic behaviors, I avoid counting. Instead of counting, I encourage her to figure out a hidden part of a whole, after looking at the whole for a couple of seconds. She seems to think sometimes really hard, her eyes focused on the manipulatives, and then sighs with relief when the task is done. She seems to look for a positive feedback, particularly when the timing matches her own feeling of self-satisfaction. Her eyes become clearer each day.

Surprising difficulties: Echolalia

Difficulties begin when we get into the question–answer activities. It kicks in after two months of intense vocabulary learning, and expanding it to word combinations and phrases. She seems to understand vocabulary words, combining words into phrases and short sentences. But when asked a question, she repeats the same question without providing an answer. She does not get the concept of a question. That it is something that needs to be answered, not repeated. The sequence "listen–think–answer" seems to be something she does not find important, even. Nothing worth paying attention to. How could it be that she understands so much about language structure already, does abstract math exercises successfully, reads the majority of words, but does not understand the concept of a question?

I decide to figure out how to communicate what "question" means. I take a few dolls, line them up on the table, facing me, create a name for each doll, make a name card and place it in front of everyone. She is sitting opposite me, so that the dolls are in front of her. I call out the name of a doll: "Who is Mary?"; I encourage her to find a name card "Mary," lift the appropriate doll up and say, "I am Mary." She has to repeat after me each time. She tries to repeat a question, but I say *No*. "Just listen 'Who is Ken?'"; then "Find Ken and lift the doll up." I encourage her again to say now "I am Ken." She repeats after me and puts Ken back on the table. Again: "Who is Margaret?" – she has to wait and not to repeat the question, listen instead, recognize the name, find it written on a name card, and lift the appropriate doll up. Next, "Who is Mary?" again. This time she already waits, figures out the name card, lifts the doll up and repeats after me "I am Mary." We keep going and she gets the game. Soon she starts to answer herself "I am . . . ." Next, I place a different colored candy in front of each doll. Now I ask, "Who has a blue candy?" She has to lift the appropriate doll up and say, "I have a blue candy." Then, "Who has a red candy?"

We take the same activities to the Piano Room, where questions and answers are created and the differences emphasized in musical questions and answers. For questions I use upward, and for answers downward direction of pitch sequences that correspond to words while still following my composing algorithm where the first note of each corresponding musical expression of a word is determined by the number of syllables. I encourage her to recognize the dolls by the names expressed in music, both with vocalizing the words in the questions like "Who is Mary?" or "Who is Ken?" and purely instrumental versions without saying the words. In music, I keep the musical expressions of the same words the same: for example, "Who is" sounds the same in music both for "Mary" and "Ken." The same for "I have a . . . candy" sounds the same in music while "blue" and "red" sound very different. This helps to communicate that listening to all the words in an expression is important. That just one word may require a different answer although other words may be the same. This helps to develop a more sustained auditory attention for the whole duration of a phrase/sentence, and become aware of the concept of questions and answers.

We keep playing with questions where only one word makes the difference in order to determine a correct answer. Listening–recognizing–acting–answering. Very soon, it is not hard anymore. She understands the system, and how it works. That a question includes something important that needs to be recognized, then directed to an appropriate object, the appropriate feature of an object has to be recognized, and an answer formulated. It becomes fun. And along with these activities, she learns that everyone has a name. That she has a name, and when called, she has to answer. And when somebody else's name is called, it is *not* her.

She can read most of the words written anywhere now and understands a concept of a question and answer. And most surprisingly, it has been only two to three months during which she has developed from 30 word approximations to basic meaningful vocabulary, both for spoken and written language. She reads the words without knowing any phonetic analysis. Words are just pictures like any other images. With meaning. These months seem to prove that she is able to learn and develop, both language and otherwise.

Month No. 4, April 1992

Creating a book for her that matches her linguistic level

She will be six soon. It seems to me that at this point she would likely benefit from supporting her reading skills, so she can get access to what the information written in books can provide. She reads single words whether by one or combined, but the meaning of full sentences where each word can change the meaning would be critical to work on. I quickly realize that the only way to proceed with meaningful sentence reading and comprehension is to create special books just for her needs. The published children's books don't provide the necessary steps in a manner that targets *her* current language level. I create the first book for her, accompanied with a recorded audio on a tape. I take a basic three-word sentence and then expand it. Each page has only one sentence. For example, the first page would be "Mary has a ball." I make the audio recording using a tape recorder, where I record my voice "Mary has a ball" followed by a glissando on the piano as a symbol to turn the page. I encourage her to follow with her finger each word corresponding to the audio. And then turn the page when the glissando is played. The next page would be "The ball is red." She has to follow with her finger the words corresponding to the audio again, and then turn a page again when the glissando is played. The third page would be "The red ball is big" etc. The audio with the glissando helps to emphasize the timing necessary to connect hearing, vision, and motor aspects within a predetermined timeframe. She has to speed up. First, she is not quick enough to follow the appropriate words with her finger. The glissando makes her turn the page anyway. She realizes herself that she has to speed up in order to get the words followed quickly enough to be ready for turning the page when the "glissando" sounds. She cannot allow herself not to turn the page on time or she would be lost for the rest of the book. She learns this all by herself through the exploration. She learns to speed up in responding, thinking, and acting. And she does notice new words with different colors on each page. That the words matter. That their sequence in sentence matters. She seems to get a concept of a storyline. From the first word of a sentence to the last one, followed by glissando, the new sentence on a new page – from the first word to the last again, noticing a new colored word, glissando and turning a page again etc. Until the end. She clearly enjoys "reading" this "book." And she learns that there are several sentences connected with each other, and that they may have a certain sequence.

Her sixth birthday

One day, around her sixth birthday, after four months of the intensive interaction in multiple environments and settings, we are at the bookstore again. We have been here many times before, hopeful to ignite an interest in books by exposing her to an environment with a lot of books. So that she can choose which books she likes to have a look at and possibly take home with her. Usually she has been browsing some of them, usually picture books, but really never wished to get one in addition to these she had at home. This time it's all different. She picks up a Walt Disney comic book, a periodical. Once she opens it, she cannot take her eyes off the pages. The rest of the world seems to stop for her at this point. She is examining the book so thoroughly and so intensely that we can hardly leave, the book still open in her hands. Walking down the street, her eyes are still in the book. I don't stop her. I don't tell her to wait until we get back home. I just make sure that she is safe in traffic. I let her be. With her book. For as long as she wishes to. She discovers something in the world that she is so interested in. That makes sense for her, excites her, makes her to want more. Now that she is able to read the words and say them out loud, she can explore what previously had been inaccessible for her – anything to do with language. She can read and articulate what the characters are saying to each other, despite her vocabulary and other language skills not being developed enough to understand the linguistic meaning of what the characters are saying. Not just pictures and characters and text. But how they progress in relation to each other. Everything in the comic book is in sequence. Pictures in sequence. Emotions and body language of the characters – also in sequence. Like three parallel worlds, all in coordinated sequences. She can figure the meaning out from the pictures with characters' exaggerated body language and emotions. I don't realize yet how important this find – the series of Walt Disney comic books – becomes for her development, including overall understanding of the world, language, speech, emotional and social development for the next couple of years or even more. Each month when a new volume becomes available, she gets the next chance to explore, discover, connect, figure out, memorize, develop her language and understanding of social relations further. She memorizes instantly everything in these comic books: the characters, what they look like, what facial expressions they have on each page, what they say to each other in relation to how they look, the page numbers and volume numbers. She equips herself in a continuous manner with phrases and sentences in relation to the social situations shown in the pictures. And then applies these ready-to-use phrases to real life. She actively tries to find appropriate situations to use these phrases and sentences with a highly emotional voice. For example, she could say when referring to a car in the street: *"This one's the wrong color! Got to have one to match the scenery!"*

To my great surprise, she seems to express the emotional feeling of the situations in the book in her vocal expression by matching the degree of the exaggeration with the body language and facial emotions of the characters in the book. I have never read these books together with her. There is no way that she is copying me. She somehow creates these highly emotional vocalizations of the verbal expressions by herself. Surprises me on a daily basis by suddenly responding to something in everyday life in a rich and expressive language. When asked where she learned that particular speech expression, she provides the exact volume number and page number where this particular expression originates from, a full citation, in her answer. I am so surprised and stunned at the same time, realizing what an extraordinary memory and organization she must have to enable her to do so.

She reads. She likes to read. She is interested in reading. Thinking about what she reads. It is all different now. For me and for her.

Chapter 3

New life begins

Discovering the world beyond Legos and puzzles, 1992 spring to 1993 fall

What changed during the first four months of highly intensive multi-intervention?

These first four months – a fresh start – after returning from St. Petersburg where she was evaluated by Dr. Traugott have proved to be transformational. A sharp change from not responding to responding to another human being – *me*, her mother. From being alone and planning her own activities – lining up toys in various ways or building Legos – to asking ME to provide her "more" of the world she had been not part of previously – literacy. From acting alone to acting together. From experiencing just her own undertakings to discovering that together – *me and her* – she can discover new things in the world. That together – me and her – we can share not just toys and vocabulary cards, but also joy and satisfaction. That we can share disappointment and sadness, and that together we can find ways to always get back to happiness. During this time period from January to the beginning of May 1992 – approximately 120 days or 1440 active hours or 86,400 minutes – I had been the only person for her, being with her as a mother, friend, therapist, special educator, teacher, speech therapist, music therapist for every single moment of her entire awake time. Every moment together felt like trying to make music in a group of both advanced and beginner musicians. When advanced players are looking for the synchronization and phrasing of a joint action during a fraction of seconds, then beginners just have to be encouraged to take those first steps, so they can become interested in the activity and develop both their individual musician skills and playing music together skills. This is what the beginning of her language acquisition at this step of her development feels like. Me as an advanced player and she as a novice trying to create "music" together in a way that allows her to build her natural interest in not just *what* we do, but in doing it *together* in a manner where split seconds matter. However, this arrangement – no outside help beside the experience, understanding, and guidance of Dr. Traugott and Mrs. Golovina – has been very hard for me both physically and emotionally. Nonetheless, it has been also a strength in terms of an opportunity for us to learn to relate to each other while transitioning from *"managing" our lives by trying to control the symptoms* as we did in the early years into *creating a life* – present and future together with each other. If she had had all those specialists – speech therapist, special educator, music therapist separately trying to work with her using even the same approach and amount of time and intensity, I question whether it would have had the similar transformative impact on her unless there had been a well thought collaboration and coordination in place to address the wholeness of her development. Everyone involved would have had to be open and willing to change their interaction on the go to ensure both reciprocity and speed while working towards the same goals – relationship building leading to emotion sharing while simultaneously building meaningful connections between visual, auditory, somatosensory, and motor systems – building a foundation where language acquisition and use *can* start making sense.

What I have learned during these first critical months after returning from St. Petersburg is that learning to learn is so much more than trying to apply just a teaching method on her. There is nothing to "fix" in her. Instead, it is all about initiating, creating, building – so she can have tools to connect with what society can offer her. So she can use her true potential for her own development and participation in society. So that she can get access to both human connections and previously created human knowledge. Like any child, but under difficult conditions. She needs the tools in order to be able to discover what *she* can offer to others while getting something in return. It feels like we have already established a foundation for life, a new and necessary beginning, a creation of *we* – me and her together like other children and their parents. When we started, her capability for joint attention seemed to be just a few seconds. And now, just a few months later, step by step, I seem to have become a partner she can expect always to be there for her. Her partner who she relies on to get new interesting puzzles for her to be solved so she can figure out the solutions.

Her partner with whom she can feel joy *together* when she has successfully solved a problem. A partner with whom she has common interests. She seems to have just discovered that there are more interesting things in life besides Legos and the like but she needs *me* – her mother – to help her to be provided with them. This is how it feels to me when we return for our second visit to Mrs. Golovina in April 1992 to show what we have achieved so that new guidance for further developmental activities can be provided.

How did this all happen during just a few months when none of it had seemed to be possible before – for the entire five and a half years? It is as though I and everyone else had tried to communicate with her not just in an unknown language but also in a culture foreign to her. What she responded to was *not* what everyone had expected her to do – by attempting to teach her just words so she could start using them for communication – saying words and phrases to her while looking at picture books together – a truly impossible setting for her recommended by speech therapists. She did not respond to the verbal story telling approach that speech therapists recommended then and still do – 25 years later – for children with minimal language. It is no surprise to me that every third child still fails to acquire speech using this approach. My understanding is that in order to respond to the verbal "storytelling method," a child has to be developing in a manner where the non-verbal/preverbal affect-laden communication already exists, and that just a story itself is missing. Verbal stories and storybooks created from a typically developing standpoint did nothing to help to connect my daughter with me or ignite interest in her for years – "looking together and talking" activity as a means to learn language failed. What are these items in a picture supposed to tell her? How to look together into a book that she has no interest in? How is it even possible to look into a book together when she refuses to sit in anyone's lap or even close proximity so that this activity becomes possible? This approach couldn't serve as a way to develop communication and language with her since the foundation was missing. Too many years had been lost due to a recommended method that she didn't respond to.

What she *did* respond to was making myself present in her life in creative ways that connected me with her both physically and *emotionally*. What she responded to was inviting her to join me in exploring the world in ways that engaged her emotionally by igniting her interest and requiring her to engage in thinking patterns similar to what she had mastered while building Legos and solving 1000-piece puzzles, leading to her feelings of self-satisfaction and pride. *Interest* is one emotion that had emerged spontaneously and allowed for *confidence* in a narrow segment of her life. I realize that her Lego construction and puzzle solving has not been just her special interest or activity. It's her strength as a way of communicating with the world, a set of "pre-language" visual/touch/motor skills, her own "language." However, communicating through Lego building or traditional puzzle solving didn't work to build a connection between me and her and develop language. She was not interested in joint building Legos or solving picture puzzles. She did it fully by herself and faster than I ever could. Clearly, she was working with her own ideas, planning and executing and didn't want anyone to stop her flow of thoughts and actions. This part of her I understood – I would have been not able to feel joy and satisfaction when playing piano or violin with someone constantly interrupting. However, the difference between her and me in a creative process while being very young was that she was aversive to sharing it with anyone while I wanted to be heard and listened to, and admired.

I come to the realization that contrary to many professionals who seem to be continuously under the impression that she is incapable of learning, she has *already* developed into a specialist in comparing, categorizing, recognizing patterns, and using these skills effectively to build and solve. But I also realize that without helping her to build access to language and communication she can keep perfecting her building and solving skills but wouldn't be able to connect these with the world more widely, missing also what the world has to offer her. So, what I have learned so far is that her preexisting "language" of comparing, categorizing, and identifying patterns proves to be a key to connect with her – communicating through the way of thinking she has already developed and understands, the medium where she has learned to operate by herself and where her *confidence* in her own abilities already exists.

As expected by Dr. Traugott and Mrs. Golovina, her behavior has changed dramatically during these critical months as a result of developing interest and satisfaction in literacy learning while expanding her capacity to focus on her renewed interests and developing her sense of self. When she is engaged in figuring out things – there are no behavior problems – no rocking or running away like before. Her thinking and engagement seem to bring peace and organization to her mind. She doesn't have to be forced to make eye contact to make a connection – when she is interested in connecting with me – in order to get a new interesting thing to solve or share her emotion – her eyes meet spontaneously and increasingly frequently with mine. However, it doesn't mean that she can keep her good behavior up when she has nothing interesting and new to discover, solve, explore. It takes her just a few seconds to turn into her rocking behavior. In order to keep her interests up, I learn to recognize the moment that signals her "fast developing boredom" – just before she begins waving her body and head rhythmically from left to right. I learn to catch that "moment" and quickly hand her some new puzzle, language or math workbook wherever we are. Keeping her interest and engagement up serves as a strong and reliable natural behavior modification.

What I have learned about her spoken language learning so far is that speech sounds were not the sounds to start language learning from; they didn't connect with her. Speech sounds didn't help to link her with me emotionally and therefore couldn't lead to speech development – these meant nothing to her. But violin and piano sounds did. Before meeting with Dr. Traugott, I didn't know how to use her responding to violin and piano playing to advance her language learning. Although Dr. Traugott didn't give me any particular ways to use music for language learning, her general understanding of "no attention to sounds" and "no meaning attachment to sounds" in the children she had studied enabled me to make that connection – using her preexisting attention to violin and piano sounds for connecting with her via sound and developing it further to connect written language with spoken so she can learn communication via spoken language. To connect visual language learning with spoken language, she needed to be introduced to the sound world where she can engage her thinking similarly to visual problem solving – using the "language" she knew already as seen from her Lego creations and puzzle solving – comparison, categorization, pattern recognition. Words as melodies with timbre contrasts, pitch fluctuations, and rhythm variations. Music proved to be critical for making connections between written and spoken language. Music brought life to communication between me and her – enabled us to fill the words with emotion and help to communicate the concept of an acoustic form of spoken words in a timely manner – a pitch and rhythm contour, dynamics in loudness and duration.

What I have learned about developing a connection between her and me is that the *way* I respond to her – my facial expressions, my tone of voice, my body language, the timing, intensity, and duration of all of it in relation to her and in relation to my verbal response – proves to be of utmost importance. It's not really about getting her motivated to learn language just by putting stars on the board when correct – we have not done it at all. It is about genuinely sharing those special moments so that her feelings become my feelings and my feelings amplify her feelings so that she can develop her sense of self. Working with her is really like making music together – it's not about just playing notes. As what is in between the notes makes music sound music, the connection between her and me while she figures out the relationships between the vocabulary cards, picture cards, and toys is what makes the development of her sense of self and learning possible.

First, it was just for a fraction of a second when our eyes met – always right after the exact moment of her feeling "relief" when solving something I had given her, the special moment when the intense focusing, the tension on her face and body is followed by letting that intensity go. First, she experienced that moment of "resolve" – maybe for a second, not more than two seconds. I learned to catch those seconds instantly. I learned that when I respond during that exact moment with showing my facial and body language how happy I am that she got it, and that she is happy about her own result, her feelings about self-satisfaction and pride get amplified. Like in music making when one person plays a phrase and the other joins in within a split second, matching the phrase but increasing its dynamics while providing additional timbres. Sharing the process of music making results in more powerful music – not just more notes but the shared experience between the players. I learned that she notices my exaggerated "join-in" and turns her eyes towards me. And then I noticed that she started looking for my response by seeking it. I realized that I was becoming her mirror. That she is making her first steps in seeing and valuing herself through me. That how I look and feel, may become an integral part of her. I come to the realization that from now on, I have to consider my impact on her at every moment. When she sees herself through me like she has just shown she does already, the way I am around her becomes very important. I have to always handle myself in a way I want her to become. The way I see myself in the world may easily become how she is going to see herself in the world. I cannot allow myself to think negative thoughts and feel down – it's going to become a part of her too. What I can do is to think ahead and configure my "mirror" response in ways to influence her in a desired direction. Although hard, I learn to switch off from negativity around us, mostly coming from family members or professionals not believing in her, so that I can be also that protective wall between her and those who are not willing to open their hearts and minds for her. I also make sure that she is surrounded with beauty. Her comfortable soft clothes with colors she likes and texture that feels good for her, organized home with fresh flowers, good freshly prepared food, candlelight for breakfast, lunch, and dinner – it all seems to have a calming effect on her.

Now, after those four months we have spent every awake moment together while learning to learn from each other, she is reading, acquiring not just basic vocabulary but already phrases and sentences, looking increasingly frequently into my eyes, expecting me to share her happiness and provide her with interesting things to figure out – this dramatic change would have never happened when the approach to teach her anything – including language and communication – didn't change dramatically as well. From trying just to talk to her, just saying words and sentences to her – to experience life together so that we can share what we both have lived through together.

From reading to speaking

Discovering the Disney comic books in the fourth critical month changes the way we have been learning so far. There is no need for speedy uninterrupted presentation of language materials to keep up her interest anymore. She is interested in her language development herself now. She reads the comic books, memorizes all the situations, their sequences in parallel of full phrases and sentences. Even the facial expressions of the characters. Her pronunciation improves dramatically in a very short period of time. She seems to get the information from the written language to help distinguish between speech sounds. Clearly, she is using the reading capability she has just developed to learn spoken language. What is most surprising to me is that she articulates the language that the characters share with an appropriate emotionally expressive tone. Is she translating visual emotional content into vocal characteristics just naturally or has she memorized previously the emotionally rich vocal patterns without having access to the words themselves and now just matches words to the speaking tone? She has always responded to my violin and piano playing, and birds singing. But not to words. I have never read these comics books with her, so it is impossible that she has learned from me how to connect emotional tone appropriately with the phrases and sentences in a book. She decides herself when, what, and how to read. It is her own world. I just buy the comic books. She decides what pages to investigate, what to memorize, and what to say. And *how* to say it. She tries to match the situations in the book with the situations in everyday life, figure out what the words and expressions mean more widely. This is where I step in – to adjust and shape the meaning of a phrase. These books have become a vehicle to learn rich language in a written form which is synchronized with the sequence of moment to moment happenings presented visually in a comic book, and connect this language with the real world. At this point, she is using ready-made phrases and sentences from comic books in her speech – such an upgrade from just 30 word-like vocalizations a few months ago.

Discovering that sounds in the environment have meaning

Our visits to book stores, toy stores, coffee shops, restaurants become more frequent. These provide us opportunities to explore different environments together. While doing so we both experience the same situations simultaneously that creates a common basis for sharing. Without experiencing together, I would find it hard to communicate clearly to her what sharing is about. Creating instant memories enables us to react to what's happening around us in a split second *together*. We look into each other's eyes as we see and feel a variety of things. We both put sunglasses on when the sun is bright. We both put more clothes on when we feel cold. She picks one book from the shelf at the bookstore, and I pick another. I ask her to show me her book and I show mine. We make different decisions and then compare. Whatever she pays attention to, I find a way to share something about it both nonverbally and via spoken language. I translate whatever is appropriate to the current situation into simple language right there, whether in a store or in the street, or in a restaurant using only the words and their combinations she can easily understand, helping her to pick up on meaningful reciprocal communication via language. I am trying to show her what life looks like and feels like when people share their experiences not only nonverbally, but in language.

One day, when we walk in the center of a city with lots of traffic, she suddenly reacts sharply to some traffic noise and asks, "What is that sound?"

She is asking a question! And the question is about a sound! She has turned towards me and is waiting now for me to answer! This question doesn't sound like one from a comic book. It seems so spontaneous. I answer what I think is the sound she is referring to. She responds by nodding her head and vocalizing "Aa-ah," using the downward directed pitch in her intonation – like thanking me for clarifying it. We are having a back-and-forth spontaneous communication! We are finally having a real conversation!

As it appears she has never paid attention to the kinds of sounds that are common in heavy traffic, a similar situation keeps repeating.. She keeps asking about sounds around us in the city. I keep answering. Sometimes I cannot be sure whether I am detecting the same sound, but I keep trying. She is connecting to the sound world where sounds have meaning. There is a source of these sounds. The intensity. The duration. The timing. Sounds convey information.

Visiting the art gallery

One day I take her to the art gallery. I would like her to see the beauty of the paintings that look different from hers and introduce her to the world of art. I am also wondering how she may react since she seems to have extraordinarily good visual perception. Her own artwork shows that she pays attention to visual details, including proportions, angles, colors.

We enter the gallery. She shows her best behavior – quiet, peaceful, focused. It feels a right place to come to expand our horizons – I think. I don't direct her in any way. I don't communicate with her much – I let her feel the place, the building, the exhibition halls, the silence, how space is used for displaying art. I don't attempt to talk to her. I just let her be. She starts immediately to look at the paintings. Surprisingly, she seems to have a system how to approach these. Her eyes move from left to right starting from the upper left corner, her gaze going horizontally to the right, and then jumping back to the left. Level by level. Making sure that she doesn't skip any area of a painting. Each painting. One after another. It takes forever to finish just one exhibition hall. First I am standing just behind her. When I realize how deeply she is involved in investigating the paintings, I decide to move to a distance away. We end up spending two hours in the gallery. During the whole time she is just looking at the paintings. What exactly she finds so interesting – I don't know. She looks so advanced in this environment. What an ability to focus. I am impressed.

Math

Math has quickly become her favorite activity besides comic books. It provides her with an opportunity to explore, connect, and figure out life without words in a systematic manner. I am keeping language out of the math exercises as much as possible as recommended by Dr. Traugott and Mrs. Golovina. If she learned math through language that is underdeveloped, she would have to develop mathematical thinking within the limits of her linguistic development and would not be able to use her mind freely. Her beautiful Lego creations have revealed her advanced nonverbal thinking patterns despite her underdeveloped language. Clearly, her language skills are not representative of her true intellectual capabilities. So, it would be not just very difficult for her to build math skills via a linguistic approach like is usual practice with the typically developing children, but it would be an unreasonable approach. Exploring and discovering connections between numbers themselves and the numbers as representatives of connections in nature do not require linguistic knowledge. In the number medium, she can use just numbers and their combinations, and how they connect with each other without "translating" it into another system – the linguistic one. Although math skills can be acquired nonverbally, the importance of those skills in the development of abstract thinking seems substantial, particularly when reasoning within the linguistic medium is challenging. Developing cognitive skills in any way would hopefully help her to grasp language more easily and boost her confidence. As both Dr. Traugott and Mrs. Golovina stressed, math enables her fast intellectual development, which otherwise would depend mostly on her language acquisition. Therefore, math is critical for her. Both reading and math are her saviors.

As recommended by Dr. Traugott, we never count like most children do – "one-two-three-four" etc. Counting can turn into an automatic activity where thinking is not necessary like her rhythmic vocalizations "A-aah" and "E-eeh" had been. We want her to engage in thinking. We want her to solve problems. We want her to get excited about solving the problems. And we want her to feel pride and satisfaction. So that she can develop her sense of self.

In order to encourage her to think about quantities, I use small sets instead of singular items. This enables her to identify the quantity visually without verbal counting. Verbalizing numbers and quantities is a separate/additional activity but not the basic one. She learns the basic words only after she has acquired a concept. The concept can be expressed in words only after understanding it. Not the opposite way. Always thinking before expressing. So, initially, I present math problems to her in a way that entails visual identification of quantities – without actual counting – only as the first step towards solving a problem. Reaching the final solution requires her to determine those quantities that are hidden from the visual view. This way she is encouraged to involve both concrete and abstract forms of thinking simultaneously. For example, I present her two sets of items – the coins – within two equally sized circles. For one set, all the coins are seen, but for another, some of the coins are under a cover. The nonverbal visual message is that since the two circles containing coins are of an equal size, the number of coins within each must be the same. On the left she can see all five coins, but on the right, she can see just two coins but not those hidden under a cover. She has to decide how many are under the cover. So she has a visual quantity of five on the left and her mind has to subtract two from five in order to reach the decision to drag three unseen coins into the picture. Instead of counting "one-two-three-four–five" and hopefully "learn" a number line while doing so, she is encouraged to engage in multiple simultaneous cognitive processes right away. Just by presenting this visual exercise, she is invited to "notice" the following: (1) both circles are the same size; (2) differences between quantities that are visible on the left and right; (3) a partial cover on the right circle. Then she is encouraged to "determine" how many coins are not visible under the cover on the right. She can use help from the left circle where all five coins are seen. This simple exercise entails not just a concept of a quantity of five, but also that five is made up from lesser quantities – two and three or even other possibilities, and that there is a way to make both sets equal. This exercise expressed in language – whether spoken or written – calls for many words and sentences. It demands a good linguistic understanding in order to grasp what this is about. She doesn't have that yet. However, the same exercise visualized looks very simple – just two circles with a total of seven coins, a cover and a question mark on the cover and a few coins on the side ready to be dragged. Just a problem to be solved.

She looks fully engaged during math activities – a thinking look in her face and a pencil in her hand when she keeps doing an exercise after another, then a page after another. Very soon, she switches from visualized problem-solving exercises to written abstract math herself without any need to "teach" her or guide her. Interestingly, she doesn't seem to be afraid of large quantities like many children are. Whether it is 9, 90, or 900, she seems to know the difference. Larger numbers seem to be her special interest that provide her with more options for manipulations. Math seems to speak to her in a way she understands. It looks like she has her own special language for having conversations with numbers and symbols. She seems interested in those conversations – the exercise says "80 + 20" and she answers "100." Or the exercise says "80 + ? = 100" and she responds "20."

She seems to have no difficulty or confusion when the similar exercises that were first visualized in pictures, are expressed in an abstract form – just numbers and math symbols. It becomes clear that for her mathematical development, she just needs an access to math workbooks so she can explore and discover the system of numbers and mathematical signs. She can do math independently when presented in a systematic and hierarchical way. For me, it means that I can have some "Me" time. She can work by herself on exercises for a couple of hours without a break, during which time she typically can finish the amount of the same exercises children in the first and second grade do over a few months. I am surprised: how easily she has grasped so many concepts during such a short time; how easily she manipulates numbers and connections between them; how easily she started to use abstract math – just numbers and symbols instead of picture problems. The amount of work she can do without a break is astonishing. I realize how important it is for her to just get an opportunity to develop without restricting her in any way. I never stop her before she stops herself. No school would ever provide an opportunity for six-year-olds to get engaged in math exercises for two hours in a row! Moreover – I cannot find mistakes in her work. Never. I don't know how exactly she thinks when figuring out the solutions. I can only decide according to her answers that are always correct. Math becomes a highly calming activity for her – she becomes fully organized – switching on her intense thinking for long periods of time. It becomes an activity she is looking forward to. It starts to serve as a reward for which opportunity she agrees to work on sentence structure and grammar problems that she doesn't like so much. It also means that we hardly leave the house without a math workbook in my purse so I can quickly provide her with a calming activity when she gets overwhelmed. The math workbook becomes a way to modify her behavior. I learn to recognize those few seconds preceding her rocking activity – a timeframe when I can prevent it. Being in public, I quickly grab a new math workbook or a new small portable puzzle from my purse to get her immediately into thinking. Adding and subtracting numbers in a workbook, working with proportions, money, puzzles – it brings peace. When she is engaged in thinking she is calm and organized.

Math and language in public

We keep balancing inside work with being in public, so she can learn to use her new language and math skills for her own benefit. As stressed by Dr. Traugott, creating opportunities for her to use her newly acquired vocabulary in real-life situations where she can feel the usefulness of communication via language seems to be an important component of her development of her sense of self. It's more than just using a word, phrase or a sentence in an appropriate setting in an appropriate time using appropriate eye contact and body language. When she has an opportunity to experience firsthand that she has a power to make her own wishes come true – this is how she learns the value of the communication.

In addition to going to book stores, toy stores, grocery stores, one particular cafeteria becomes our favorite – a café where she has to use her newly acquired language to ask for whatever she desires. She can buy chocolates or other sweets here, or order a meal. She seems to like her freedom to choose from so many good things what to buy for her own money. Sometimes it takes her a very long time to figure out the pros and cons of the combinations of the items before she proceeds with buying – this is how it looks when I observe her from a distance. I make sure that she has all the time she needs. I don't intervene unless necessary.

I also open her a bank account so she can have new opportunities to experience the benefits of communication, but also planning. In order to make her wishes come true, she realizes that she needs to get money. When she goes to the bank she has to communicate her banking needs to a teller in order to get money. She learns about what money means in a systematic way in a real-life situation while becoming her own manager. She also learns that she can use only what she has – the concept of limits. Getting a bank card with her name on it makes her feel very important and proud – she feels she is like other customers in the bank.

The usual sequence of her thinking/actions is: she gets an idea of what she wants – a particular treat or a toy for example; then figures out whether she needs more money than she has in her wallet; if so, she asks me to take her into the bank. I stay usually at a distance so she can fill in the form necessary for withdrawal – the amount she decides by herself. Then she asks me to take her to the cafeteria/restaurant or a toy store she had in mind to get what she wants. She looks serious and grown-up when dealing with money. Since children are not seen every day in her bank, she is treated very well by a teller. She seems to like to communicate with a teller – handing her or him her bank slip and her bank card and receiving money while making an eye contact with a teller. Every time that I observe her in this situation I realize how important it is to provide her with these real-life opportunities from which she can develop independence.

Puzzling interpretation of her nonverbal IQ score of 146 by a child psychiatrist

Age six, March 1993

When she is six years old, a year after our visit to Dr. Traugott, we have been asked to participate in research at a local university that is just beginning to look into autism, a condition not known among medical professionals here before. I agree to take part in the study. I fill the extensive questionnaires about my daughter's behavior to be sent to the Autism Research Institute in California. Our participation also includes taking a Leiter intelligence test that is administered without oral language. Since it doesn't require verbal instructions or verbal responses, it is considered more accurate than other tests for children with language problems.

For the Leiter IQ test, we visit the university psychiatry clinic. The test is administered by a child psychiatrist but I am allowed to be in the room and observe. Although my daughter knows how to read, write, do math and have a simple talk with another person, she refuses to say a word to the doctor. She doesn't know what this situation is about. She doesn't know what to expect or whether she would have any interest in being here. But otherwise she behaves well and agrees to sit at the table when asked to do so. The test begins without any speaking or other ways of interacting. The doctor is placing the wooden blocks on a frame in front of her and she just starts to manipulate these. She immediately grasps what she has to do just by looking at how these wooden blocks are arranged. She seems interested in doing this. She looks serious, a thinking look on her face. The doctor keeps placing new combinations of the wooden blocks in front of her and she keeps manipulating these in a certain way. She keeps going without any break in her attention until the test is done. I am amazed how interested she is in this activity, how she likes to solve problems. Problems that she recognizes visually. I am also amazed how long she can keep her attention up in an unfamiliar and new setting when she becomes fully engaged in thinking. While observing her I find myself thinking that I have to provide more of this type of activity for her. When done, we leave. I will have the results in a few days.

The Leiter nonverbal IQ score is 146. I am relieved. For the first time ever I have an objective measure to back up my observation that she is a talented child who just has to be helped to develop so she can connect with the world. I feel empowered and eager to do whatever it takes to give her the opportunities she needs. She has a very high potential and we just have to keep going.

However, after revealing the result – the score of 146 – the doctor doesn't seem to think that this Leiter nonverbal test gives an objective measure about her, since it is nonverbal and doesn't take into account her verbal abilities. Now suddenly it doesn't seem to matter to the doctor that she is reading, writing, doing math with numbers up to 1000 at age six. I am puzzled since before the testing the same doctor considered this test perfect for her. The result "146" has apparently changed the doctor's mind. However, I don't pay so much attention to the doctor's surprising interpretation of the test result either. I already know what she has been able to do within a year and now I have this number – an IQ score of 146. This is what really matters to me.

The doctor provides a name of the school suitable for her next year. I even feel good that there is a school in existence for her because I thought that there wasn't. My feeling is that this school must be specializing in children with high nonverbal intelligence who have language problems.

Within a week I am visiting the school that I don't know much about. I meet with the headmaster. I learn that this is a wonderful school with a low teacher/student ratio, that most of the teachers are special educators, and that they provide such a good care and education for the children. I want to know how exactly. Now I learn that this school is for children with low intelligence. Those who may not be able to learn to read and write, who don't understand math. These children have an opportunity to come to school every day. They are provided with care and special education.

I leave. She will not go here. I feel not just disappointed but offended. Knowing more than ever that my own decisions about my own daughter are the only ones that matter. That the way I see her may determine her quality of life both in the present and in the future. And also mine.

It is impossible for me to understand the thinking behind the decisions of the child professionals who don't find reading, writing, math, Lego building, high nonverbal IQ important while determining a child's educational needs. It feels like the professionals find my daughter to be unfit to participate in society at large regardless of her already acquired high level skills or her potential. They seem to see her "mental age" still at the level seen in two-year-olds and forget that two-year-olds don't read, do math, build complicated Legos, solve 1000-piece puzzles. They have chosen not to acknowledge her already highly visible strengths while considering her weaknesses not worth working on. They seem to be doing everything in their power to make sure that my daughter wouldn't have access to what every other child seems to have – an education that would enable her to find her place among her peers and reach her full potential.

The family reactions to her success are puzzling too. While my own family shows sincere happiness regarding my daughter's remarkable advancement, my extended family members and friends who had previously formed their low opinions of her seem to be unwilling to change their negative attitudes. It's like "good that she reads but this doesn't matter much." More surprisingly, I learn that some who knew our situation well actually feel very uncomfortable that my daughter reads and their children don't. I had not realized that there had been such a social hierarchy in place – that many had felt actually good that my daughter had such a problem so that their children of similar age looked so good compared to mine. Now the "higher ranking" of my daughter's reading ability that everyone can easily see is causing other people to feel uneasy.

Her father, who has been continuously profoundly influenced by his family and had previously formed a negative opinion, even feeling victimized by us, seems to be torn. He seems to not allow himself to embrace her remarkable transformation even if he would like to. He sees that our daughter reads and finds it good when asked, but fails to recognize the significance of it or chooses not to do so. He hasn't seen most of our work in action since he has been out for most of the days during these four criti-cal months. But he has never shown any interest in our activities either. I have tried to show him, asking him to be part of it. But he has created a wall already that I cannot break and he is reluctant to break. He is highly influenced by his parents, particularly his mother who doesn't think that her daughter-in-law – me – does anything right. Therefore, in order for him to join in with us in the developmental and communicative activities, he would have to build another wall against his parents. It has happened a few times that he came suddenly home while we were still working. Surprisingly, seeing us working as a team evoked more negativity in him towards both of us than ever before. He looked upset, even angry. The fact that our daugh-ter is learning, communicating, sharing has not been enough to change his previously formed negative and hopeless attitude. Moreover, when he hears me praise our daughter for something, he starts accusing me of giving too much credit and having a false hope for her. "Be realistic about her" and "she has not earned a praise" – the common phrases I hear over and over in an emotionally charged tone. His message is clear to me – he is afraid of her getting better.

Similarly, my mother-in-law keeps expressing her dissatisfaction with me – that I give unfounded credit to our daughter, and that I spend too much money on her developmental materials, that I take her frequently to restaurants, cafeterias, and other places where we spend money instead of keeping her home, which would be a much cheaper way of living. She always finds me guilty – whether not doing anything for our daughter's development like before we visited Dr. Traugott, or doing too much now. Somehow I still believe that in the bottom of her heart she must have the best wishes for her granddaughter, and that she just doesn't know how to separate her own fears and shame from what is in the best interest of a child, her granddaughter. I am astonished that the whole family of teach-ers with such a potential to help have chosen their role in their daughter's/granddaughter's development only as being "harsh critics" of both a child and her mother without realizing how detrimental it is to the wellbeing of a child. They organized taking her away from me a few months before we ended up in Dr. Traugott's home in St Petersburg. It didn't work out – I have forgiven them without being apologized to. Have they not been able to get over their feeling that I must have been the reason our daughter didn't develop like other children, and therefore, they cannot accept that I am the one who has been able to actually change her developmental trajectory when no one else did? I was supposed to be the guilty one, and their son the one who is saving our daughter from me. And now, just over a year later, when things are so different – they cannot acknowledge that they had been wrong. It seems to me that this may be a reason they have not showed interest in becoming an integral part of their granddaughter's discovery of the communicative world she didn't know before. Ironically, my daughter has an opportunity to learn from them that not all of the communications between people are pleasant. For me to see so closely how the best interests for the child don't seem to matter within a family is shocking. They stick to their belief that I still am doing everything wrong. They keep accusing. I hear that I am spoiling her by praising her for her work that is not good enough – that our daughter should be praised only when she has acquired fluent speech like other children have. Anything less than that she has not "earned." I am puzzled. For some reason, at this point I still keep thinking that getting our daughter better will positively affect how her father and his parents, our daughter's grandparents, particularly my mother-in-law, and other members of the immediate family perceive her. It doesn't happen. It feels to me like that "when our daughter gets better *because of me*, her 'guilty' mother," they cannot accept it. Just recently they wanted to save her from me by taking her away, so how can they suddenly start supporting our developing relationship that has already has led her to reading books, the skill they had thought she would never be able to acquire? Instead of getting her more books to read, they continuously keep their blame game up. What has been missing is a simple question I would have so much appreciated – "how can we help." Joining in – this is what I have been expecting. It seems impossible. I don't know it yet but they will never change their attitude about her whatever she achieves in her life – three languages, a graduate degree, fully independent work, home and leisure life – even these will be not enough to earn praise or congratulations or just simple contact in any form in her future life. The only change they are willing to make is replacing their verbal accusations with silence, indifference, and distance. Within a couple of years my daughter will be fully excluded from all aspects of their family life. She will lose the whole family from her father's side, but she will be freed from having to face their negativity towards her.

We keep going without knowing what the destination may be. We have no other option than just to live our life by keep filling the days with new explorations and experiences as we have done already.

Her seventh birthday

By our daughter's seventh birthday, she has acquired the academic content of the first and the second grade through our continued home intervention. She reads, talks in sentences, does math operations in multiple digits, behaves well. Language is limited, but it exists, and it's functional. She makes lots of grammar mistakes when she speaks and writes, but math – this is a subject she seems always to get right.

She already has gained access to literacy and information via written language – reading. Her vocabulary and language structure continues to develop fast through independent reading – comic books and encyclopedias. Understanding spoken language is still a major problem. She needs to get accustomed to the voice of a speaker, speed, and flow of speech, and she needs to be provided with a context beforehand so she can understand more easily what is said. New people with different vocal timbres pose a substantial problem. When speaking, which doesn't happen easily with people she doesn't know, she uses unconventional word combinations, which frequently affect how she is perceived. Language-wise she can be looked at as a foreigner who has learned some language, has trouble understanding but can communicate a lot if necessary. Interestingly, many keep asking, including doctors and nurses, what country she is from. She looks like an outsider. The first impression she seems to give to others who don't know her is that she is a foreigner, and not that she has some medical condition. She is highly motivated and eager to learn new things. Everybody her age is going to start school in September, and she wants to go to school too. For me, it seems that it is time to introduce her to the life of other children her age. Her academic knowledge is two years ahead; it's time for social development – she has enough language to do so.

One day in spring, the headmaster of our local school decides to visit our home unexpectedly. He says he would like to discuss how to arrange one of their teachers to come to our home twice per week next year to provide education for her. We have never contacted the local school regarding her education. Why has the school already decided without any discussion, parent involvement, testing, specialists' evaluations – a usual path for children with special needs – that she cannot attend the school? He doesn't know about her success during the past one and a half years. He doesn't know her at all. But somehow he is already convinced that excluding her from her peers is a way to go. His decisions and actions must be based on what he has heard from people talking in the neighborhood. Clearly, the local school is interested in having her enrolled since their state budget depends on the total number of children in school. So, as it appears, they want to enroll her without allowing her to come to school. They want her and don't want her at the same time from the school's point of view. But she needs other children. She needs to learn how to become a member of the society where the relationships matter. She needs to have an opportunity to experience the social aspects of development, which cannot be learned without being among others. She needs to compare herself against others, feel the emotional dynamics in the classroom, adjust herself to others.

The truth is that we have not even considered the local school for her education. The primary reason is the lack of consideration of emotional development in public schools. She needs a kind of school environment that respects the essential nature of childhood where the emphasis of learning is on building a foundation for social, emotional, cognitive, linguistic, and physical development – every component being equally important. She needs a school environment built around the understanding that young children think in doing and experiencing, and express their feelings in action. She needs a school environment where the innate creativity of children is honored and acknowledged as the main building block to enable learning. For her, it would mean that her creativity can easily serve as a tool for establishing primary communication of thoughts and feelings, so that language can become a meaningful way of communicating the same thoughts and feelings in a different way. She needs a school where she can develop socially and emotionally and measure herself regarding her academic achievements against others. She needs a school environment where educators understand how our lives are shaped by our surroundings and respond accordingly at the moment-to-moment basis to create, recreate, and sustain the optimal learning environment. She is affected by feelings around her tremendously without being able to use words to describe these yet. When she experiences negativity around her, not necessarily towards her – like two students talking to each other with an emotionally charged vocal tone using exaggerated gestures, or a teacher responding to something with disappointment expressed both in facial emotions and body language – she feels anger and fear without knowing what this is about and without knowing how to respond or whether to respond. She can easily become a prisoner of her own feelings triggered by feelings of others and will be not able to develop.

It's my deep understanding that the classroom environment the children are exposed to must support in every way the very same vision we have for our children's future. What children experience shapes their mind. If she enters a school among children who are not typically developing, she would learn that the way these children think and act is how she is expected to think and act. If she enters a school among typically developing children but where children are measured by how they fit into the educational standard and not by how they contribute to the community in their classroom, she may feel undervalued and learn that she does not fit into the society. This is why the school choice feels like being of utmost importance. She has experienced the home environment where emotions and feelings were addressed as foundational for academic learning, a basis where learning can be built on. Candlelight breakfasts, lunches and dinners, music, art, fresh flowers, comfortable clothes, lights and sounds that set a stage for peaceful but intense learning have become a standard for her. We are looking for a similar environment in school for her where beautiful surroundings, art, music, poetry, and teachers with high emotional intelligence shape the everyday environment children experience. Everyone can learn academics outside of school, but learning how to become a member of the classroom community, to contribute and to receive, cannot be taught without experiencing it in the classroom setting.

A local public school doesn't provide these qualities. The surprise visit from the headmaster suggesting a school-centered solution that excludes the contact with other children and the school building speaks for itself. Even the art classes and music classes are considered out of reach for her. There is no reason even to try to negotiate since the understanding of human development is profoundly lacking in this school.

Introducing social development and independence: going to school together with typically developing peers

A private school becomes my first choice and my husband, who still is my husband at this time, agrees. It seems that the only idea our daughter's father and I can agree on, is a particular private school, founded a couple of years ago by parents who didn't agree with existing education standards, which ignore the emotional and social development of children. These parents hold a belief that the educational environment, the way children are developed and are talked to becomes their inner voice for the rest of their lives. The school they decided to establish is based on Rudolf Steiner/Waldorf pedagogy where creativity, play, storytelling, poetry, nature, art, and music are embedded with the academics. What I like most is that this approach ensures that children experience the social aspects and musicality of language – through playing games and reciting poetry while in a circle, and doing eurythmy, a form of movement that links language and music in body expression. These aspects of development seem just so right for our daughter at this point in time.

This way I also follow the recommendations of Dr. Traugott that she has to be among typically developing peers – in a social environment where she can have exposure to the ways her peers communicate with each other, so she can experience firsthand how social connections form and have an opportunity to become a part of the community of her peers in natural ways. Anna's vocabulary of 30 word-like vocalizations at a time when we met with Dr. Traugott a year ago seems a distant past. Now she responds to her name, reads, speaks, does math, communicates in a bank, buys her own treats. A year ago the discussion with Dr. Traugott about how to integrate Anna among her typically developing peers seemed more like a dream, but now, just a year later, it makes so much sense to me. Both Dr. Traugott and Mrs. Golovina had stressed that she is going to school not to learn academics primarily, but for the social purposes – the aspects of her development that are not possible without being among her peers. Academic knowledge can be acquired individually, but not the social development. Typically developing children provide an environment where she learns from her peers how they interact with each other – the role model for socialization. Mrs. Golovina provided further recommendations how they have worked out a model to make it work in a school environment. She stressed that it would not work if she was just dropped off in a regular classroom. She cannot become a distraction, a problem either for teachers or for other children – that would be damaging for the class environment that we would like to be a role model for her. Also, teachers cannot be expected to teach her in some special way. That would be both very hard if not impossible from a teacher's point of view who have to be there for all the children equally, and her becoming "special" who needs extra attention and help would alter the class environment in ways that don't allow her to become integrated naturally among other children. She has to feel as one of others, and not the "special one" among others. In order for her to establish herself as one of others, she has to feel good about herself in something. She has to feel confident in some aspects of her being there, so that other aspects – the social ones she is lacking – can become integrated with her preexisting strengths. In order to make it work, the teachers need to know that her academic development is already ahead of her peers and that she is going to be prepared for the academic content used in the classroom beforehand anyway. So that when she enters the classroom in the morning she already knows what this will be about. Only then would she be prepared to measure herself against her peers, notice how others are doing, get a feel of herself among others, establish herself socially.

We meet with the school officials and realize that they have a say who they admit to their school. Both parents and children have to be a good fit, share the philosophy of the school so that children are supported appropriately also after school and holidays. Home and school have to work together. The school is for typically developing children – it is important that she is not a distraction to others. I explain the situation and emphasize that it may be the only school where she can take her first steps into socialization. I explain that academically she is well developed but needs to learn how to be among other children in a supportive environment. I emphasize that she will have all the support needed from home. She is asked to come to meet with the prospective teachers privately. She looks good, behaves well but doesn't talk at all during the assessment. The main teacher, whose specialty before learning Waldorf pedagogy was special education, cares deeply about children's development. She decides to give her a chance. I understand deeply that we can't demand anything for her from school. We can just try to help the teachers so everyone involved feels good and safe.

In September, at the age of seven, she goes to school. The first day. She stands in a line together with 25 other children waiting for the teacher to open the door and shake each child's hand to welcome each child separately saying their name and wishing good morning – a tradition in Waldorf pedagogy. Children seem to feel so important and organized during this simple handshaking procedure. The same every single morning.

She is one of the children being as important as everybody else. She seems happy and proud and is eager to go to school each morning. They have free play; they go outside each day, they eat at a communal table where organic freshly cooked food is served and good table manners expected.

However, she does not speak for the first two months. But she is not asked to speak either. She is allowed to get accustomed to the school environment without any pressure. She joins in with other children for every activity except speaking. She knows how to speak but avoids it. Then they start to learn poems. The teacher provides me the texts of poems to learn at home with her so that she is prepared. Everybody else learns these at school. At circle time when they recite poetry together, accompanied by the rhythmic movements, she starts to speak finally – by reciting poems together while doing rhythmic movements together. She is one of other children! She has an opportunity to be like everybody else! Soon the teacher decides to let her read a book – a fairy tale during the circle time. Since she is the only one in the class who can read fluently at this time, she takes the place of a teacher. She has an important chore now – everybody is listening while she is reading. It is heartwarming to see how reciting poems and reading a fairy tale for other children bridge her way to start using speaking for communication with other children. Frequently, I send some treats to share with other children, so that she can build the communication even more easily. I learn from the teacher that she goes and asks everybody afterward whether they like the treats.

This is the beginning of her socialization that continues in the Waldorf environment for the following couple of years.

Existing speech enables her to start speech therapy

I feel that seeking the professional help to enhance my daughter's speaking and language skills may be worth another try after failed attempts in early years. She has acquired communicative language to an extent that allows her to interact with a speech therapist now. Every opportunity to interact with others, particularly when systematically supporting multiple aspects of her language use, seems so crucial at this time when she is just starting to use language at school as a mode of communication and learning. However, finding a speech therapist who is willing to accept that language underdevelopment and an intellectual capability to develop language may coexist, is not an easy task. I am aware that speech therapists have no known methods or theories ready to use for a child like my daughter. Even setting goals for therapy may pose a problem. But I know that they can be very helpful if open to recognize a value of human communication outside the common understanding and practices of their field.

I realize that there is a subspecialty of speech therapy that addresses language issues in those who have lost their language due to brain traumas and diseases. Although those individuals are in a different situation having developed ways to acquire language before they lost it, the process of speech therapy still involves building functional language and human communication. I contact the aphasia department at a hospital. The head of the department agrees to meet with me and to hear all about my daughter. I tell her what we have been through to get where we a now at seven years of age. I tell her about auditory attention problems and behavioral issues, and all what she has achieved during the past two years – from 30 word approximations to reading, speaking, and going to a Waldorf school. Despite being past the echolalia stage and reciting memorized phrases from comic books, her spontaneous language – both spoken and written – is full of mistakes. Also, she would benefit from advancing her conversational skills in a targeted way.

We discuss whether and how my daughter's language development can be supported in the aphasia department where the majority of the patients are adults. Also, I want to know how other patients' treatments are approached, particularly of those with global aphasia. The way the head of the department talks about her patients who have lost their ability to speak touches me deeply – she has an admirable ability to view a person apart from their disease. While talking to her, I feel her genuine respect and dignity towards every person regardless of their ability to speak or not.

She assigns a speech therapist to work with my daughter. A young lady, recently graduated from the university who is open to the ideas outside her academic knowledge. She becomes my daughter's speech therapist for the next couple of years. They develop a bond – an emotional connection – that enables my daughter to be motivated to work with her. She is outgoing, full of energy, and considers the human reciprocal communication more important than linguistic mistakes my daughter makes – those are corrected always *after* the meaning is communicated. They laugh a lot together while working, and when my daughter's hyperactivity doesn't allow her to work, she sends her to run ten times back and forth in the hallway to enable her to channel her energy. She provides much needed speech therapy, addressing both receptive and expressive language in a way that my daughter feels that she is valued as a child and as a friend. The aphasia department becomes the refuge for both of us where we always feel welcome.

How a library becomes her favorite place to spend time after school

A new library in a new multi-story building with numerous reading rooms and hundreds of reader's seats, a large conference hall, a theater hall and exhibition areas become her favorite place to spend time after school. She gets her library card with *her* name on it. From now on, her interest in books spreads beyond Disney comic books – to newspapers and encyclopedias, music and art. With her ID card, she can access reading rooms of her choice, including the fine art reading room and music reading room. During the first half of a day in school her main job is to learn to be with other children, her academic knowledge being ahead of others, then in the afternoon, she can follow her natural interest towards obtaining new knowledge in the library. This also means exponential growth of vocabulary and a structure of language, reading graphs and interpreting schematic representations of various worldly information.

First, I accompany her everywhere in the library. In reading rooms I first just observe her from a distance to give her an opportunity to feel more freedom, but ready to support her if necessary. As it appears, she doesn't need my help. Being just close by seems to be enough. She learns how everything is organized in the library by herself – by observation. She likes to choose books from a shelf, browse these and then return to a designated book return shelf. She notices that there is a separate shelf labeled "Books for return." Then she discovers that she can also access books that are not displayed – by ordering these from catalogs. She notices how the books are organized in a catalog. That there is a system. That there are several systems. The ordering process itself involves not only finding a potentially interesting book from a catalog and filling out an order form, but also an interaction with a librarian. Here she has to both talk and listen.

She seems to like all that structure – showing her ID to get into the library, taking an elevator to a certain floor, choosing a reading room, browsing through catalogues, filling out order forms, taking these to a librarian, checking whether her orders are ready for pick-up, exploring the contents of ordered books, and then returning these. In this library, books and other materials can be read only in the library in person, these cannot be taken home with her. She educates herself how to find information about the books and from the books. All the help she seems to need from me is accessing this extraordinary environment – a library.

In addition to learning new things about life from books, she appears to like the calmness and freshness that the thick walls of the new building provide, along with a peaceful code of conduct everybody follows. She likes the environments that are quiet. She likes the buildings that are new and don't smell bad. This new building enables her to enjoy herself. It seems to be all she likes – peaceful, quiet, very clean, beautiful, and provides endless opportunities for her natural curiosity. She seems to adjust her way of being to the general atmosphere she sees around here while observing other people. The days that she didn't know that it matters how she behaved among others seem to be behind us. Usually, there are no other children, only adults. She seems proud being that seemingly only child interested in what the library has to offer. And she is always noticed and greeted warmly by the staff.

Soon she comes up with an idea – she asks me to go to the cafeteria so that she can be by herself in the reading room. We agree that she will be at the cafeteria in 15 minutes – telling her an exact time like 4:15 p.m. to meet me. She has a watch on her wrist, and she knows how to use it. I go to the cafeteria leaving her by herself in a general reading room. In exactly 15 minutes she enters the cafeteria. I am relieved. I give her some money. She goes to the line with other people to buy whatever she likes to eat. To get what she wants she has not only to talk, but talk in such a way that she is understood.

Next time it will be 30 minutes by herself, then an hour. She is always punctual meeting me in the cafeteria. It feels like building trust step by step. I trust her to be by herself in a reading room and then show up at a prearranged time at the cafeteria, and she trusts me to be there at that time. She learns the meaning of trusting. I trust her so that she can enjoy her freedom and independence, and she knows that she has to live up to it. She trusts me to be in the cafeteria so that she can find me when she wants. Her watch becomes more and more important for her – it enables her to experience both the freedom to do something by herself until the time is up and the security that at a certain time she will connect with me again.

One day she tells me that she had gone by herself to another reading room – the music room. She had ordered some classical vinyl records and listened to the music in a particular chamber. She had handled all the records, the equipment, earphones. What a surprise! She has become so independent.

After a while I feel comfortable dropping her off in front of the library with some money to use in the cafeteria, and then pick her up in two hours – her waiting, ready to be picked up at the time we both agreed. There are no cell phones yet, so everything has to be prearranged with her and then just followed through. The library becomes the source of both knowledge and independence, and a safe, beautiful, peaceful, and pleasant place to be.

Since she is communicating more and more via language now, I learn about sensory issues I had noticed but had not been aware of how deeply these were affecting her. She is able to express now that she doesn't like certain places like restaurants because of the sounds knives and forks make when they touch porcelain plates. This is why she had preferred hamburger restaurants – not because of hamburgers themselves but because of the different sound environment these had – no high pitched noise of metal cutlery when it becomes in contact with porcelain plates! Also, she reveals that she doesn't like the sounds of electronic toys – we even have a picture showing her covering her ears and having a very painful look in her face when her father is dialing a toy phone that makes high pitched sounds each time he presses the numbers. There are two other children younger than her in the picture who both seem to be fine with these sounds, only *her*, a child who had been considered profoundly hearing impaired is the one not tolerating these sounds. To protect herself from unpleasant sounds, she has started recently to use a hair accessory – a headband – that enables her to cover her ears immediately when necessary to diminish the impact of unpleasant sounds. Surprisingly, it happens very frequently. She expresses also that she doesn't like the speaking voices of some people. She even draws a graph to show the sharp acoustic peaks some people create when they speak while others speak more evenly. I realize that it is mostly due to the "s" sound. Also, she is able to express now that she prefers really soft and pleasant clothes. I learn that her favorite color is blue and that she hates red. It starts to make all sense now – this is why she was covering her ears frequently and demanded only soft clothes and preferred those to be of the color blue.

Chapter 4

Coming to America becomes a window to the world

Middle school

It is Monday, December 1 1997. Her first day in school in America. She is excited and looking forward to be enrolled in the 6th grade. The grade is so important to her. The 6th. Her 1st language – both oral and written – is functional by now, but with a lot of grammar to be still worked on. Her second language – English – is limited to a few words and expressions. She wants to discover how it feels to be with other children from many countries and different backgrounds in a school environment. She had learned some English in a summer camp at one of the public schools in the area when she visited a few months earlier. So she has some experience. She wants a fresh start. A possibility to succeed. In an environment where nobody knows her. And where her past is past.

Her American schooling has not been planned or even hoped for. A few months earlier, after a two-month summer visit to the US, she returned to Europe, so that she could continue her education in the same language that she was already using actively for communication. This was a theory that made sense. In practice, it didn't work out. The previous year, she had to change schools – from a Waldorf school to a public school when she was under my mother's care while I was studying and working in the US after a painful divorce. My expectation had been when my daughter's behavior improved in parallel with language acquisition – her lack of language was the most basic accusation towards me by her father and his family – then they would accept her. I was wrong. The more our daughter's behavior, language, and communication skills improved, the worse her father's attitude towards her and me became. A typical day for me started as highly enjoyable, filled with more and more hope each day as I observed our daughter developing not just language, but her sense of self. This all ended every single night at the moment when her father came home and started accusing me of ruining his life. The accusations became increasingly intense – his trying to convince me that not just *him* but *everyone* else who knew me – all our friends, family members, neighbors, even my sincerely thankful patients – hate me and feel so sorry for *him* having to put up with me. One night I couldn't tolerate it any more – at 1:30 a.m., in the middle of his nightly aggressive accusations, I took our daughter and left. This ended our relationship forever. He was free from us and we were free from the overwhelming and intolerable negativity and aggression.

My mother became my helper when I needed it the most and supported me in any way she could. Soon after I came to America to study, my daughter's school change became inevitable – she had to leave the Waldorf school full of arts and creativity and go to a public school in another city where her talents were not recognized and supported. Another Waldorf school in the city I had hoped for her to go to refused to take her – a decision made after a short in-person meeting with her. The only public school that agreed to allow her into one of their classrooms was a special school for those with movement disorders and other serious health issues – many children of her class were using wheelchairs.

When she returned from her summer visit to America to start in the new school in September, it appeared that she had to repeat the grade – despite her academic results having been the highest during the previous year. The "well-meaning" and "caring" head of the school wanted her to be "on the safe side" – by preventing her from being exposed to new knowledge that may possibly lead to academic difficulties. What the head of the school saw as a way to success, meant the opposite for my daughter. She didn't understand it. It did not make sense to her. She had not been assigned any "remedial work" for summer as had been a usual practice for children with academic troubles – she had the highest grades after all! The head of the school explained to her that she did not have enough knowledge for a foreign language class – English – and not enough math skills to proceed with her peers. She agreed that she had minimal English, but she was good in math! Math had been her favorite subject, a language where words were not needed. She had been doing abstract math since she was five to six years old. Math had been her strength and identity, her savior from the verbal world, a medium where she can freely think and express herself. How could it be?

It seemed that the general understanding in the field of education had been that for a child with language difficulties, it is automatically assumed that math must be an issue too. Language has been historically considered as an indicator of intelligence. The problems in language meant for many that math would then be even more problematic. Not in her case. She made her first steps in learning math as a symbolic language in parallel with language learning. It's just another language for her. No one seems to think that a foreigner cannot do math in a country where he or she does not know the local language. Math is like music, a language understood across the cultures. So, she was deeply offended by the head of the school, an educator who never checked her math knowledge, but who knew without checking it that she must have problems in math because she makes mistakes in grammar and sentence construction when communicating her thoughts. My daughter realized at her deepest level that whatever she achieves – even the top grades – is not enough to prove to these educators that she is capable of learning.

After two and a half months trying somehow to tolerate the schooldays with her classmates who were all younger than her, with nothing new to learn, knowing that the teachers don't believe in her, she is eager to return to America. She wants to escape. I understand. She is 11 years old and now she is ready for her third transatlantic trip as an unaccompanied child. She has become so independent, that spending eight hours on an airplane under the care of a flight attendant who can be reached with a touch of a button from her seat, is not a problem for her in exchange for getting out of that intolerable school situation. While educators find her incapable of learning at the same level with her peers, as a world traveler she does better than most of the children her age. She has experience of learning her first language under extremely difficult circumstances – as a foreign language without being based on any preexisting language – so crossing the Atlantic on a plane compared to the difficulty of language learning would not be an issue. She gets all the coloring books, puzzles, and candies. She has a passport with *her name* on it. Her name that she had learned only after she was already five years old. Having her own passport makes her feel proud and important. This is what she seems to need the most right now – a feeling that she can do exciting and important things in her life despite the people around her who still seem to think she is incapable. Her classmates have not been to America, but she has. Her classmates have not traveled by plane by themselves, but she has. Her classmates may not even have passports. She wants opportunities where she can test herself. She knows the feeling of satisfaction when she achieves her own goals. She wants to experience this feeling again. It would have been impossible in a school system where nobody believes in her.

So, she is about to go to school in America. I feel that it is like throwing her into deep water without knowing whether she can swim. There is no way to predict how she is going to handle it. There is no test in existence to evaluate truthfully which educational and social setting is right for her other than giving her a chance. I have been trying to communicate to the school counselor beforehand that she has sensory issues and that she is a differently developing child. However, I have avoided the term "autism" since behavioral problems have not been a problem for a few years already. The last incident of any kind was during her second year in the Waldorf school when she had hidden herself in a closet. Her teacher revealed that they had used a new high-pitch metal percussion instrument in the music class when it happened – high pitch sounds were the ones she has been so sensitive to. It is unlikely that any other incident like that would happen again – she has grown so much since then.

Also, I have been warned by my American friends that bringing the label "autism" into light may mean bringing prejudice into her life again. However, I want to be sure that the 6th grade is appropriate for her. No question, that the best school environment for her would be a mainstream school. Her primary goal for being in school is to learn from the social environment – as recommended by Dr. Traugott at a time before her language development took off. Having been her primary educator and therapist, I know that she can advance academically beautifully in a home setting or with a private teacher, or in a school like Waldorf with lots of arts and music. How would she do in a new environment – a school in a foreign country among typically developing peers? One thing is clear – she cannot learn to adapt socially without *being* in a social environment. So, the question really is which grade would be right for her here? According to her age, she would be in grade 6. She had finished a 4th grade last spring and was now repeating it again despite her top academic results. She would have to "jump" from grade "4" to "6" to be among her peers of her age. Could it be a reasonable switch considering that she is in a new culture – new language, new ways of doing things, new ways of thinking about things?

She wants a chance. I feel I need to look into what the children in America are actually doing in grade 6, so I can understand whether her capabilities would allow her to take a chance of successfully skipping the 5th grade in addition to the major cultural change. My research colleagues who have children of the same age kindly show me the work their children are doing in school. This enables me to assess the academic level she would be exposed to in the 6th grade. What I'm trying to evaluate is whether she would be able to understand the concepts involved. I am not worried so much about the different ways of doing the work at school. I am concentrating purely on an intellectual level necessary to understand. Knowing how she thinks and how she learns, I don't find anything I have been shown that she cannot understand conceptually. So, the 6th grade it is. Together with the children of her age. In a mainstream local public school.

For Language Arts she goes to the ESOL (English as Second Language) class. The children there have just recently arrived from different countries. Everybody seems to feel equal to each other – an extraordinary opportunity to begin a new chapter in her life without the baggage of negative attitudes by people around her. A new environment where new connections are made. Without past. Hopefully, some friendships will be established. The teacher is extraordinary. The teacher connects with the children and cares about them. The teacher teaches English to all these kids with different native languages. My daughter likes it. She has already had the experience – of learning her first language as foreign. She advances at an extraordinary pace. Without any help from me. She is doing so well – according to her own feeling *and* according to the teacher.

Math. Not surprisingly at all, her early acquired nonverbal thinking patterns seem to allow her to "jump" from 4th grade to 6th in math without even noticing it. What it actually means is that instead of doing simple additions and subtractions as they did in the 4th grade just a month ago in Europe, she is calculating percentages now in America. She understands. She enjoys the feeling. She doesn't need any extra help here at all. She loves that she can do it at a new level where she has to think more than before. Math allows her to establish her power. She notices that there are children in her class who don't understand math so easily as she does. This gives her an opportunity to start helping out her peers from the ESOL class – a good start for establishing friendships! She sees herself as good in something compared to others in the 6th grade. Despite having skipped the 5th grade altogether! Her self-confidence grows day by day. In a few months I receive a letter from the school that they have observed my daughter together with other students and have found that she is above grade level in math and would benefit from a placement in a newly established advanced math class next fall. This letter is the first document I've ever received that says so clearly that she is doing something very well.

Science is harder. It is language based and she doesn't fully understand what the sentences mean or what is wanted from her in the class. She just tries to keep up. This is a subject I am helping her with after school but my help is limited to language and a general understanding of how the science class works. We discuss what the sentences and expressions in her science project descriptions mean. The language in the science class is different from anything she has ever seen. It is nothing like the comic books or encyclopedias that she loves, or even novels that she doesn't like. Understanding what is meant by those complex sentences as a guide for what to do in the class is where she needs help. I "translate" the complex sentences into a simpler language that she understands and point out what she is expected to do with that information. While general verbal communication seems to have taken off nicely, writing descriptions and results in science is difficult for her – expressing the content in the form of a paragraph so that others understand requires organized expression of thoughts in language within the subject of science – a situation she is not familiar with yet. We are working on it together.

What seems to be really important is that she is looking forward to going to school each and every morning. She is developing in an extraordinary space – both socially and academically. By the spring, her second language – English – has developed to the level that allows her to explore the news by reading newspapers and how things work in the universe by reading encyclopedias. She can access world knowledge now! A bookstore close to our house becomes her favorite place to stop by after school. She typically spends a couple of hours there each day – just browsing through books. Among her favorite choices are the ones related to politics, presidents, world leaders, physics, astronomy, chemistry. One day, she asks me in a serious manner – what I have done for humanity. I don't know how to respond, so I ask for her clarification – what does she mean by that? She explains that like Princess Diana or Mother Theresa – what are my contributions to the world? Knowing now what she means, I answer – "raising you."

When Mother's Day approaches in May, she hands me a beautifully wrapped present she has bought with her own money. I feel through the wrapping paper that there is a book inside. For some reason, I'm sure that this is a Disney comic book. When I open it, I am astounded – the book she has chosen for this very special day that celebrates me as her mother, the person who has become the closest of anyone to her, the one person she has truly learned to rely on is *The Seduction of Hillary Rodham* by David Brock!

She keeps surprising me – both by her thinking and her actions. Soon I learn that she is planning a birthday party with her friends – this is what she calls the four girls with whom she has spent a lot of time together in the ESOL class along with other subjects. At a time when she is telling me about her wish to throw a party, it appears that she has already invited her new friends in person. Moreover, I learn that she has finished creating the invitations too. These are beautifully designed and crafted and she is ready to give those to her friends. I am amazed. I open one – it reads "Please come to my birthday party at 3:11 p.m."

Her thinking and planning her own birthday party is so unexpected to me. I had been thinking that I would ask her in the near future whether she would like to ask some of her classmates to come over to celebrate her birthday. And then I would have planned it for her if she said "yes." Before I was ready to address her upcoming 12th birthday, she has already claimed her ownership of initiation, planning, and execution. The only thing that I truly end up addressing is her planned unconventional beginning time of the party – she agrees to change it from 3:11 p.m. to 3:00 p.m.

I have been trying to give her independence in many ways so she can explore making decisions on her own behalf. This level of her doing exceeds all my imagination. Trying to protect her from possible disappointments like friends not showing up when expected, I offer my help to contact their parents. But she insists it's not necessary – they all agreed to come. She was right – at 3:00 p.m. on her birthday the girls arrive. I am touched to my core. At the deepest level I know that she has already opened a new chapter in her life where the existence of friends becomes more and more important each day.

The communication with the teachers during these first months in the school has been of utmost importance. Although my daughter is behaving well now, she doesn't listen continuously to what teachers are saying – her lack of auditory attention can be interpreted wrongly in various ways. I understand that teachers need to feel safe when a different child they don't know anything about is in their class. Although I feel strongly that everyone has a right to be included in society, have access to language, education, books, cultural events, opportunities to develop, and reach their potential, I also understand that I cannot demand or force anyone to like my child. But this is actually what matters the most – my daughter knows intuitively when someone is thinking in a negative way about her. Without saying the actual words expressing their doubts directly to her, people reveal their thoughts via facial expressions, body language, movement dynamics patterns, tone of voice – she detects those more easily than anyone expects from her. She does her best only when surrounded by people who believe in her, are positive about her. Individuals around her not believing in her are her worst enemy. Therefore, the idea that I would demand special treatment for my extraordinary child in school as a right is unthinkable to me; it would ruin everything I want the school to be for her. My understanding is that the only way forward is to do everything in my power to connect with the teachers in a positive and constructive way to assure them that my daughter's academic development is fully supported by me. So they wouldn't be worried about how to teach my daughter differently from others. From the teachers' perspective – they want every student in their class to succeed while they really cannot become a private teacher simultaneously for 20+ children in the classroom. From my daughter's perspective – she needs to feel equal to other children in the class and that would be possible only in a classroom where the teacher–student and student–student relationships form naturally. I feel it is my job to communicate to the teachers that my daughter's learning capacity is based on her extraordinary visual strengths combined with her high level thinking in *her way*. I feel that it is my job to invite the teachers to see my daughter's strengths being extraordinary. I feel that it is my job to convey that I am an expert here. That I am not just supporting my child, but expanding the teachers' understanding of child development generally. The major goal for my daughter is to participate in class, an opportunity to advance academically in a social environment. Allowing her to use her strengths her *own* way instead of trying to make her adopt someone else's ways of thinking seems to be of utmost importance to be effectively communicated to her school. I provide emotional support, and I am ready to support my daughter's academics if it becomes necessary – I make it very clear to all her teachers and administration. In January, just a few weeks after my daughter took her first steps in the school in America, her teachers express their concerns whether she belongs in a regular classroom during a meeting. In May, just a few months later, the decision is made, both at the school and county level, that she doesn't have an educational disability and can continue in a regular classroom! She has been able to make everyone believe in her.

Skipping a grade instead of repeating it, changing continents that expose her to much that is unknown instead of trying to keep her in familiar surroundings, switching to another language instead of considering it harmful for a child with language problems, all happening within a six-month period, has worked for her benefit against all odds, becoming a crucial stepping stone, an enabler for further development. Without giving her that chance we would have never known that she could do that.

From this point forward, she is surrounded only by people who believe in her, support her, admire her, and encourage her. The Atlantic Ocean serves as a barrier that doesn't allow negativity from those who don't believe, and very likely will never believe in her, to re-enter her life. She likes going to school, working towards academic achievements and enjoys being with her friends. However, it becomes very important to her that she also likes all of her teachers. As it turns out, during the first week of each next school year – both her middle and high school years – she evaluates her personal connection with her teachers. When she determines that there are teachers she doesn't like for some reason, she asks the school counselor to change her class so she can be assigned to another, more favorable teacher. When I ask her, she doesn't give any explanations other than she just doesn't like that "particular teacher." I am wondering whether the reason why it seems so important to her is her history of negative experiences with her father and his family, and the school principal who made her repeat the grade – the people who found her incapable of learning. Whatever the reason, she seems to be extraordinarily determined to take charge of who she would like to be her teacher whenever possible. Knowing that a school counselor is there to help her, she feels free to go to her and ask her to make that change for her. To my surprise, the counselor always finds a way to grant her wishes.

One day, still in the middle school, she comes home upset. It appears the ESOL teacher has made a mistake with her grades – somehow a "C" has ended up being her grade when it actually belongs to someone else from her group. She looks very disappointed, offended. She feels she has been treated *very* unfairly by her favorite teacher. She asks me to contact the teacher and tell her to remove that "terrible mistake" she cannot tolerate. Although I see that my colleagues at work personally make sure that their children are treated fairly by teachers who grade their children's work, I feel that for my daughter, it is a perfect opportunity to encourage her to stand up for herself. Her deep feelings about this "error" may help her to initiate that "unpleasant conversation" with her teacher. So, I say to her that it is her responsibility to go to the teacher and ask about that "C." I am making it very clear: "When you want to remove that wrong "C" from your grades, you have to tell your teacher, if you don't, the 'C' will remain there." The next day it's done. The teacher apologizes for her mistake and thanks her for pointing it out. She is happy. And I will never again hear requests to contact any teachers on her behalf.

Her friendships with other children develop further. In addition to enjoying spending time together, doing girly things, going to birthday parties, and sleepovers, she discovers that there could also be misunderstandings between best friends. Her first ever experience of serious misunderstanding with one of her friends affects her profoundly. She doesn't know what this is about, what happened, or that she needs to do something about it. She is just distressed and seemingly in emotional chaos. Fortunately, she shares it with me – and yes, she has two languages to choose from to do so! Every time we talk, I remember the times when we didn't have either a need or a luxury of language to share thoughts and feelings. So I explain to her *in words* how important it is to understand her friend's point of view of the same situation. I invite her to think with me to figure out how her friend may have interpreted the same situation and how her friend may feel. And compare it with what she is feeling. When I explain it, she seems to understand that there are two sides in a relationship and that she may need to always consider how her thoughts and actions may affect others in addition to how others affect hers. I realize that she probably expected everyone to be like me or other caring adults in her life who always support her no matter what. Now she is suddenly in a situation where she realizes that her friendships with her peers are different – that she has to both create and keep these friendships.

In the 8th grade she has chosen to join the school orchestra. She has signed up before telling me. This is how seriously she wants to learn to play a musical instrument so she can practice and perform in the school orchestra like other children do. She doesn't seem to think that she has to discuss it with me beforehand or ask a permission. She has already chosen an instrument – a clarinet – to be picked up from the music store. This is where she needs me – to pick it up and pay for it. During the concert at the end of the year concert I cannot believe what I am seeing and hearing – she is maintaining her attention during the whole concert – following the conductor and adjusting her timing to be in synchrony with everyone else. In addition to using her extraordinary visual skills here as usual, she combines these so effectively with her auditory and motor skills while playing together with others. She starts exactly when she is supposed to and she finishes her part exactly when she is supposed to. She alternates her attention between the conductor, reading her music on the music stand, her own playing and playing together with other children. She is one among everyone else – all connected in music. I am deeply touched. While her grandmother didn't find her suitable to be included in her orchestra of four-year-olds during her early years, here, in America, she gets that chance. I am very thankful for that.

High school

Reaching high school means that she leaves behind some of her friends, teachers, and counselors she knew plus the building where she felt good since it was newly renovated and therefore, smelled good – a very important aspect for her. In the new school she has to be evaluated for possible educational help again. Her auditory attention is a continuous problem – she needs time to adjust to each person's vocal timbre and way of speaking in order to understand what is said to her. When a teacher is speaking in a way that emphasizes high-pitched speech sounds – like the consonant "s," she may not be able to understand the words since the high-pitch sounds take over while the lower-pitched speech sounds are muted. Her high-pitched hearing has finally been confirmed, so I know now for sure what I had suspected all along – that she has a particular ability to hear very high-pitch sounds – a situation that means that she hears a highly distorted speech where some consonant speech sounds are perceived very loudly compared to lower pitched vowels. According to her, she hears the high-pitch sounds all the time – that explains her good attention to birds, whistles, whispering, violin in early childhood, but in order to hear the lower-pitched speech sounds she has to pay extra attention – she has to actively listen. She has stated that her hearing comes and goes, but this concerns only lower pitches; high pitches are always there without the need to switch on listening.

Her counselor suggests special education services to her, but she declines these – she says she doesn't need special education services, she just needs education. However, she agrees that in the language-based subjects like History and English she can have a captionist in the classroom who types all the auditory information happening in the class into the computer system so that she can follow anyone speaking in the classroom visually at all times by looking at the laptop computer placed in front of her. In this setting she can truly concentrate on doing her classwork.

Like others, she takes numerous AP courses, International Baccalaureate Math, Chemistry. In Computer Science she is the only female in the class. She studies a lot, all by herself. The projects are large and require her to do her homework for hours, typically finishing after midnight. She is so determined. However, her English writing skills are much less developed than one would expect considering her high intelligence. It is still hard for her to express herself well in writing in a way other people write. The county offers her a private teacher who starts working with her during the English class every day in a separate room following the same curriculum covered in the regular classroom. She goes to the classroom only to give her presentations in front of her peers. She connects very well with her private teacher, who is very patient with her. Word by word, sentence by sentence, paragraphs are finally starting to look like they should. Writing is one of the very few areas that she didn't grasp well by herself – she needed that extra intensive help on a regular basis to learn to express herself systematically in language.

Her friendships seem to flourish. She has both a best friend and other friends. She goes to school events, sleepovers, or just hangs out with friends. She performs with her clarinet at a huge event at school – I write music for her and supervise her practicing. This is her solo performance – she looks confident on the stage while playing the music I wrote for her. The time has come to discuss and visit colleges. I can easily imagine her as a biologist or chemist doing experiments in a very precise manner. But she says "*No.*" She explains that she doesn't like being in a lab and pipetting something small. Instead, she would like to do "big things" like creating and designing systems – she would like to study engineering. Her SAT score in math is almost perfect.

University and beyond

The beginning of her undergraduate engineering studies marks the beginning of her independent life. Her new home is in a metropolitan area where the university she chose for herself is located. Classes, projects, professors, tests, exams, new friends. Her own life, her own decisions, planning, actions. Working hard studying engineering during the week and taking time off from studying during weekends – she joins a dance club, enjoys shopping for new outfits, goes to restaurants and movies with friends. I talk to her over the phone, sometimes visit her over there. She comes home for holidays, winter and summer breaks. Every time I hear her voice, she sounds happy, content, full of energy, and every time I see her, she looks happy, confident, full of energy, determined to change the world for the better. Although I miss her tremendously, seeing her comfortable in her own element brings me both relief and joy. Her success makes me feel successful myself.

Over and over again, I find myself thinking about how we got here – she studying engineering and my waiting for her to come home for holidays. Her believing in herself and trusting herself, and my believing in her and trusting her. Her showing high aspirations to achieve, a genuine inner desire to contribute to society, and build a better world for everyone. I can't help but feel privileged being an insider of her journey. Despite all the difficulties we encountered together, I feel I have had an extraordinary opportunity to be a part of her step-by-step discovery of the world around her.

Looking back into her early years – *I wish I knew then what I know now*. For the first five years, I was just trying to understand, hope, and manage our lives just to get by every single day. I wish I had met someone who knew what I know now during the first two critically important years of her life when I realized that something was definitely not right. I would have made different decisions about her and myself, and very likely avoided many shortcomings both at the personal and professional level. But what I never doubted was what appears to have become the most important component for making her success happen – an underlying belief that *it was possible*. When I look back and wonder how I was able to keep going while almost everyone I knew threw stones at me, I remind myself that there have been others in history who have been able to follow their own feelings regardless of other people's praise or blame. I did follow my own feelings – I felt I had no other choice. And my feeling was that my daughter's development into an independent and contributing member of society *was possible* – that I just had to find ways to enable her to reach that. No other person, whether a family member or a professional, was able to convince me otherwise.

However, I do think that I would not have felt so deeply that the emotional and physical bond between us was missing – the core of being a human – without looking for it. Having a strong musical background enabled me to see the absent bond more easily since an ability to be continuously aware and responsive to others every single moment is necessary when making music together. Feeling others through music making where emotions are shared, movements precisely timed, predicted, coordinated, synchronized, ready to be adapted within milliseconds with each other, had been a major component of my experience growing up. When I had my daughter, I wanted to feel her in relation to me, through sharing moment after moment with each other. Like making music together, at least for a few moments. These failed expectations were known just to me and were coupled with her behavior problems and lack of language development that showed on the surface being visible to others. I never thought that her lack of eye contact and joint attention, or her rocking behavior, lining up toys, wandering away from home and public places were the reason why she didn't acquire language.

Dr. Traugott helped me to understand that without emotional involvement my daughter would have no interest in anything, including learning to read, speak, or notice sounds around her. I understood the importance of it immediately – it made sense to me. The sounds must become useful for her, Dr. Traugott stressed, also the reading activities, or just my being together with her – only then would she be interested and cooperating in what I wanted her to do. Igniting her own interest in learning would become the starting point of everything else. I was particularly intrigued by the concept of attaching meaning to sounds. The sound world was my world – my absolute pitch has been all about attaching meaning to sounds, not just musical sounds or the speech intonation, but to every single nonmusical sound pattern I pick up – whether wind, teakettle, ambulance, speech etc. – all of those have their own pitches and temporal relationships between them, rhythm, loudness, and dynamic patterns that I could write down in music notation, sing or play on a piano or a violin instantly. As an absolute pitch possessor, I know the pitches, but I also have an intimate relationship with other sound properties besides fundamental frequencies, including emotional aspects of those. As long as I remember, the sound world has been always where I feel in my element. So it was so natural for me to start including auditory cognition activities combined with emotional aspects of physical properties of sounds to target verbal communication in our everyday lives once I knew how important this was for my daughter's development. I just invited her into my world. This is how reading and learning vocabulary via her visual ways, became integrated with auditory development via recognizing, identifying, thinking about acoustic features of sounds and creating those by herself – the same features that music and spoken language share. *It was not about learning to play an instrument or sing; it was about connecting with the sound world.*

I realized that for the first five years, I had been attempting to build a relationship with her without using my biggest asset – music and acoustic properties of sounds in general, while failing to use the existing communicative bond with her – my violin and piano playing. Speech was supposed to be speech and not music according to the understanding among the professionals. But for her, music and sounds became a window to sharing emotions, relating, and language use. Musical sounds and language are interwoven medium, not two separate ones. Without musical sounds, she may have never found a reason to relate and communicate. Since both music and language depend on sounds, it made sense to go beyond the widespread professional explanations and approaches to enhance language acquisition since those didn't bring the expected change in her development. We had to start looking for a means to combine music and language in a way that would enable us to build an emotional relationship.

Watching her as an engineering student excelling together with others, being highly functional in two languages by now, wouldn't have been possible without her becoming *fluent* in math, the cornerstone of engineering studies. Lego building aside, at age five, the same day she responded to her name at Dr. Traugott's home office the first time ever, she also took her first steps in math under her guidance. This is how important Dr. Traugott considered math in those children with behavioral issues who fail to learn spoken language via traditional ways despite their nonverbal intelligence being within normal limits. No other professional – speech therapist, special educator, psychologist – had ever considered math as something important for her. Looking back now, the recognition of math as being critical for her development, proved to be equally important as accessing language development via reading. Introducing math as early as possible – at the same time when taking the first steps in learning basic vocabulary via reading – was not just helpful, it established a foundation both for her intellectual development and her development of a sense of self. Math as a symbolic system is a language of logic that builds reasoning and comprehension while developing a mentally organized way of thinking. Math enabled her increasingly complicated interaction with the world directly without the need for linguistic communication. Math enabled her to recognize herself early as an individual with power. Math became her motivation, an indicator of her self-worth. Math enabled her to see her value when comparing herself with others when in school already. Math became her language – a way of communicating – where she didn't feel like a foreigner, an outsider. She just fell in love with it. As a result, math enabled her to become an individual with a highly developed sense of self – knowing what she wants, how to achieve it, working towards a goal, taking pride of her accomplishments, and setting new goals.

As I am watching her being a full and active member of the student body of her university, making friends, joining a dance club where she dances for hours each weekend, communicating with students and professors in the academic environment, I realize how important the early socialization was. The feeling of being a part of a social group cannot really be learned in any other way than actually being among others as a part of growing up like everyone else is. Similarly, one cannot become a piano or violin player without actually playing the instrument. From the earliest years, I took my daughter to various public places on a daily basis despite the hardships. My understanding had been that without being with others there would be no opportunities to learn from others, and learning to be *with* others. My attitude had been to do everything I could for her development, instead of escaping when roadblocks appeared. So, when Dr. Traugott discussed with me my daughter's placement at school with typically developing children as the only developmentally supporting option for her, I understood. I also understood my responsibilities to prepare her for that. When Dr. Traugott discussed how important it was to understand Lev Vygotsky's views of child development – how a child's mind develops through the interaction with others and the culture he or she is living in, I understood. To figure out the optimal settings for my daughter's development it was critical to understand that to learn language, to read, write, speak, think, and do math would not be enough without creating opportunities to interact with others, to be a part of the culture. Only then would she have an opportunity to create her life up to her true potential and find her place in society.

Dr. Traugott's also predicted my daughter's future during that week long visit at age five – that she would become a reader, speaker, math problem solver, foreign language speaker. Her vision about what would be possible for my daughter to achieve seemed dreamlike to me at a time when her vocabulary was limited to 30 words after years of trying. However, she emphasized that my daughter's success would be dependent on *me* – my understanding of what is involved and how I will find the way to make it happen. Having seen children with similar problems from so many cultures, she knew that the speech therapists, special educators, doctors, psychologists have no training and experience that would allow them to act towards the best interest of a child like my daughter. And if they had – they would have no opportunities to integrate the developmental strategies into everyday lives of those children in a continuous flow. Change doesn't happen through 30-minute therapy sessions – it happens through living a life accordingly. More than ever I realized that raising a child is a form of art – I had to become an artist to make my daughter's life a beautiful picture where she wants to belong – to be admired and encouraged.

Getting her bachelor's degree in engineering is not enough for her – she decides to go to the graduate school. I am not surprised that she wants more. She has a deep interest in a particular area of engineering she would like to pursue during her graduate studies. She is applying to other countries to make her dream come true. Even a requirement to learn yet another language is not stopping her. "I want to try myself out more" – she says. Who am I to tell her not to go after what she wants?

Today, she has finished her graduate studies and is working in her chosen field of engineering. She has her own life. She is highly functional in three languages that she uses on a daily basis. In addition to her passion to build a better world via engineering solutions, she likes to learn about other cultures. She has lived for extended periods in four countries, and visited more than 30 countries. Again and again, I hear that she is volunteering to organize a social event, or that she has again helped someone, who doesn't know the local language, at the doctor's office with translation. Recently, she came home to introduce her boyfriend.

Her success seems to have not changed her core personality she showed in early childhood. She still loves to build and solve, her favorite color is still blue, she still loves soft clothes, she connects to rhythm through dancing. The difference is that she is connected to the society now – she contributes to the common interest of humanity and expects to get something in return. Acquisition of languages has removed the barriers to accessing human knowledge and builds the capacity to communicate directly with others from multiple cultural backgrounds and see herself as being a part of the global society.

Anna about her early memories

I don't know what my first childhood memory is, but I remember that the house we lived in was next to a grocery store. I remember when we moved to a new house, and that we went to see it while it was still being built. I remember an unfinished bathroom that had a sign "1988" on the wall. I am surprised to learn that those memories must be from my very early childhood when I was between 12 and 30 months old.

In a new house we had a separate room for a refrigerator that was located next to the kitchen, and our kitchen had a door to the balcony. I remember a man (a guest from America, summer 1989), who was smiling all the time and who gave me pink bunny slippers. His extraordinarily big smile caught my attention. I liked the softness of the slippers, and how they felt and looked, and how the bunny ears were moving when I was running around. I don't remember his wife.

I have some memories from preschool. I remember swinging outside a lot, and that one woman sat next to my bed waiting for me to fall asleep after lunch, and that I was the only child who never slept. I also remember a moment when my mother took me out from a car seat in the back of a green car before going inside. These memories must be from a time period before my third birthday when I was still enrolled there.

I remember going to a swimming pool that was a part of a hospital. I don't remember anything about toys being thrown to the bottom of the pool to be brought up, being afraid of water, or being in the water together with my mother. What I remember is my mother outside the pool, me showering before and after, and drying my hair with a hair drier after swimming. Also, I remember that the first coach I had was a cruel woman whom I didn't like, and that later I had another coach who was a nice young man.

I remember Dr. Traugott's apartment – what it looked like. I remember that it was around that time when I discovered my first Disney comic book in a bookstore. I don't remember Dr. Traugott. I don't remember that she called me by my name or any other way, but I remember the yellow candy. I remember the city of St. Petersburg – the metro, church, tram no. 57. I was particularly fascinated by such a big number for a tram – "57."

From our subsequent trips to St. Petersburg, I remember Mrs. Golovina and her apartment – it had a kitchen. I remember the noise coming from the kitchen. One of the times when we arrived at Mrs. Golovina's house again, the first thing she did was that she asked my mother to write a word "cow" on a white card. I remember the "cow" card, and that my mother wrote it, and that Mrs. Golovina asked her to do so. I also remember that one time we left for St. Petersburg at 1:30 a.m. – this was such an interesting time to begin a trip. During that trip, I got a blue bike as a prize for doing great work with Mrs. Golovina. I remember feeling proud.

I remember the bookstore where I found the first comic book. I remember the moment I opened it. I remember how I couldn't stop reading it. I memorized every single thing there, including the page number for each spoken phrase and how the faces of the characters looked like on each page. Knowing the volume of a book and a page number enabled me to find quickly a particular happening or exchange of words between the characters whenever I wanted. I found it interesting how characters' faces changed while they were speaking to each other. I could see easily when they were angry or laughing while saying different things.

I remember how my mother didn't want to buy the second one immediately when I noticed it at the bookstore window. I had to ask her repeatedly to do so, which I didn't like. I still remember how deeply disappointed I was. I kept asking for the next edition over and over again until she finally bought it. Every month I was looking anxiously forward to the next edition – I had the previous one in my memory already. My favorite place to go became that particular bookstore. I have always known that I learned language through these comic books where the text and pictures were complementing each other. I still love these characters and remember how they talked to each other. I was living a life together with them. They taught me language and how language is used by talking with others.

What can professionals and parents learn from the developmental trajectory of my daughter?

The description of my daughter's development from early childhood to young adult – her continuous change over time in relation to the changes in her general and learning environment, including human relationships – characterizes her in a way that would be impossible via the results of any combination of standardized tests. Numerous autism researchers have asked me about her adult outcome – particularly about the scores of standardized tests designed for autism spectrum disorders. Remarkably, her journey of becoming a high achiever, as she identifies herself, seems to have no correlate yet in the statistical models created for describing individuals with autism spectrum disorders.

If her developmental trajectory had been published 10 years earlier – she would have been one additional individual to those few 167 persons with autism ever reported as having developed functional language after the age of five (Pickett et al., 2009). The process of my daughter transitioning from being minimally verbal to becoming increasingly functional both in the comprehension and use of language is well known to those few professionals who were willing to open their hearts and minds, recognize her potential for development, and celebrate her success.

Currently, at a time when my daughter is already over 30 years old, every third child with autism still fails to acquire functional language, even after receiving years of interventions and a range of educational opportunities (Tager-Flusberg & Kasari, 2013). A workshop at the National Institutes of Health in Bethesda, Maryland in 2010 brought very much needed attention to the lack of scientific knowledge in nonverbal/minimally verbal autism despite 70 years having passed since Dr. Leo Kanner described the first 11 children in his landmark paper in 1943. Strikingly, the majority of the autism studies conducted have excluded children with nonverbal/minimally verbal autism while choosing to focus on higher functioning, easier to evaluate verbal children. This practice has resulted in a gap of knowledge about non-syndromic/classic autism, and led to an unfortunate situation where increasingly frequent early diagnosis leaves professionals and parents with no other choice than to hope that the same intensive behavioral therapies that have been known to have failed at least half of the children on the spectrum for decades, have better outcomes when started earlier. These widely used almost round-a-clock therapies are based on a behavioral method that uses operant conditioning as a means to change an unwanted behavior. This method was originally created in 1970s by combining the behavior modification technique and learning theory with the knowledge of early child development prevalent at that time (Lovaas, 1977). Attempting to encourage language development, these therapies use operant conditioning to teach children who have failed to acquire spoken language naturally to articulate phonemes and their combinations in exchange for food, based on an assumption that language can be built up from learning isolated phonemes first, then combining those to syllables and words, followed by communicating the meaning. Since neither typically developing children nor foreign language learners learn language this way, it is not surprising that this approach has proved unsuccessful for those in need of special instruction in order to learn to talk, and whose non-verbal intellectual capabilities being within the normal range (Ankenman et al., 2014) would allow them to understand abstract concepts necessary for language acquisition.

Treating autism spectrum disorders has become a global concern as one out of every 160 children worldwide is affected (WHO, 2013). These children across the world grow up being continuously subjected to stigma, discrimination and human rights violations, including unjust deprivation of health, education, and social opportunities regardless of their true intellectual capabilities, the socioeconomic status of their parents, or country of origin. Strikingly, children with "minimally verbal" or "nonverbal" autism have been found to be at risk of being underestimated as they may be wrongly regarded as having little cognitive potential that typically results in a cascading loss of access to complex information and commensurate opportunities (Courchesne et al., 2015; Krueger, 2013).

The urgent need to build a theoretical framework for early detection, and redesign treatment approaches have recently been addressed (Magán-Maganto et al., 2017; Mottron, 2017). Not just heartbroken parents (Ellenby, 2018), but also numerous autism professionals have started to question the efficacy of the very same commonly used high cost "early intensive interventions" that have been considered "scientifically proven" despite questionable evidence (French & Kennedy, 2018).

Dr. Laurent Mottron of the University of Montreal has called into question the behavioral approach's underlying belief that children with autism will not learn by themselves due to their lack of innate ability and disposition to learn spontaneously. He has called for abandoning all therapies under the umbrella term of "Early Intensive Behavioral Intervention" – Lovaas' method, Applied Behavior Analysis, Early Denver model among others – in favor of strength-based education (Mottron, 2017). Instead of the decades-long practice of behavior modification through operant conditioning, Dr. Mottron proposes to improve access to written language using the visual strengths of those children to learn language as that should favor the subsequent speech development and decrease their problematic behavior instead. I cannot agree more – this is how my daughter discovered language and learned to talk – through learning to read first – while problematic behaviors disappeared without any extra effort. Reading became her lifeline – an essential tool that enabled her to develop her sense of curiosity and passion while gaining access to human knowledge and how people interact with each other through language. However, learning to talk as a result of presenting language in a written form required creating ways for her to encourage the development of her auditory cognition capacity necessary for understanding spoken language, while simultaneously building parent–child reciprocal relationship through synchronizing emotion sharing.

My experience with my daughter serves as an example for the strengths-based learning where a child's own interests serve as a basis for the development of inner motivational structure. I have no doubt that while building an emotional relationship with her, the decision to choose her strengths over her weaknesses was a mode of interaction that was critical. Her well-functioning sensory channel – vision, her already existing cognitive strengths like comparison, categorization, and patterns enabled her to acquire language through reading. That meant gaining access to written knowledge and education. The comic books opened up the ways for her to explore how communication – both nonverbal and verbal – is used in back and forth interaction between individuals. Also, comic books enabled her to visually explore the temporary sequences of spoken language that are necessary for understanding the concept of communication that had been inaccessible to her previously in traditional interaction attempts. However, her transition from written language to oral language had to be supported by learning the dynamics of nonlinguistic sound patterns of spoken language. Bringing elements of language – words and phrases she learned through reading – into a nonlinguistic sound medium enabled her to develop sensitivity to acoustic stimuli like pitch contours, melodic contours, rhythmic patterns, timbre variations that typically developing infants learn to respond to and imitate during the first year of life before they say their first word.

My daughter's developmental trajectory that includes the discovery of her true capacity to learn when supported accordingly – to form close relationships, acquire language, communicate nonverbally, verbally and in a written form, to plan and execute her actions – supports a recently proposed view by Mark Johnson of University of London that autism is not appropriately described as a disorder of neurodevelopment, but rather as an adaptive common variant pathway of human functional brain development (Johnson, 2017). In order to bring a meaningful change into the lives of the families of those children with autism who have been considered traditionally "unteachable," an interdisciplinary approach seems to be of critical importance. No single professional field in isolation – whether medical, speech pathology, special education, behavioral therapy, music therapy, psychology – was able to provide a way of thinking, guidance or intervention my daughter needed in order to succeed in developing to her potential. It is time to revisit what we truly know about how a child mind develops in typical development, so that this knowledge can serve as a guidance for pediatricians, speech therapists, special educators, researchers, music therapists, parents while structuring and identifying the components of the contents for research, clinical practice, and interventions to help children with atypical development like those with minimally verbal autism.

Part II

Commentary on two remarkable journeys

One therapeutic for Dr. Diana Thielst and Anna; and one of discovery for psychiatry and psychoanalysis

Chapter 5

The recognition of autism as a developmental disorder

In 1943 Leo Kanner, working at the Harriet Lane Pediatric Clinic of The Johns Hopkins Hospital, published a seminal paper on Autistic Disturbances of Affective Contact. In the paper Kanner described 11 cases of children whose early severe disturbances differed from any previously recognized condition. Prior to Kanner's paper, scattered cases had been described but the descriptive patterns that constituted a syndrome had not been formulated. In 1949, after seeing more than 50 similar children plus knowledge of many others coming to him from worldwide sources, Kanner gave a definitive description of early infantile autism as a pathological developmental syndrome. The:

> characteristic features consist of a profound withdrawal from contact with people, an obsessive desire for the preservation of sameness, a skillful and even affectionate relation to objects, the retention of an intelligent and pensive physiognomy, and either mutism or the kind of language that does not seem intended to serve the purpose of interpersonal communication.
>
> (Kanner, 1949, p. 416)

The disturbance, though commonly misjudged at first, is apparent as early as in the second half-year of life. The infants seem unusually apathetic, do not react to the approach of people, fail to assume an anticipatory posture preparatory to being picked up and, when they are picked up, do not adjust their posture to the person who holds them. They shrink from anything that encroaches on their isolation: persons, noises, moving objects, and often even food. They seem happiest when left alone. Persistent lack of responsiveness raises doubts about the child's hearing acuity. When it becomes obvious that hearing as such is not impaired, poor test performances lead to the assumption of innate feeblemindedness. This succession of a first diagnosis of deafness and a second diagnosis of mental deficiency is almost invariably a part of the case histories of autistic children. It indicates that a disturbance of relationships has been recognized by the parents from an early date.

(Kanner, 1949, p. 418)

In 1944, Hans Asperger working at the University Paediatric Clinic in Vienna, independently described the same type of autistic child as had Kanner. Asperger emphasized "oddities of non-verbal communication: eye gaze, gestures, posture, voice quality, prosody, and word choice" (Frith, 1992, p. 10). Both Kanner and Asperger describe children who avoid eye contact, and are seriously limited in their ability to socialize, communicate, play imaginatively, and understand the point of view and emotional state of others. Their attention, interest, and competence turn to physical objects, manipulating them into patterns sometimes with outstanding achievements.

Since the independently arrived at findings of Kanner and Asperger, two trends have evolved. One is to question if they are describing an identical disorder or separate entities with the "Asperger syndrome" constituting a subgroup of individuals better at communicating linguistically and more successful in adaptation. The second trend is to regard each as representing a spectrum of lower or higher functioning individuals. For example, autistic spectrum children vary greatly in the age at which definitive symptoms are recognized. Some neonates like Anna evidence unresponsiveness to caregivers immediately. Unless the caregiver or consulted professions are knowledgeable observers, the unresponsiveness will go unrecognized until later. For other infants, autistic spectrum signs do not emerge until later in infancy. The time of language acquisition and usage may differ greatly ranging from those who early acquire many words however odd their phrasing to children like Anna who are mute and unresponsive at the age of five.

Kanner's approach

In 1956 as I was completing my years of psychiatric residency training I spent a brief period with Dr. Leo Kanner at Harriet Lane Pediatric Clinic. One experience with Johnny, a five-year-old boy with an autistic syndrome disorder stands out in my memory. I first took a history from Johnny's parents. I then "met with" Johnny, who alone in a playroom, was sitting on the floor perpendicular to the door so that with his peripheral vision he could see me enter. As per Dr. Kanner's instructions, I entered the playroom slowly. Without speaking to Johnny or attempting to make eye contact, I observed him as he sat rigidly looking forward and down as he picked up lint from the carpet. As soon as I saw an indication of tension in his body and movements I plopped down on the floor paralleling his posture and began picking up lint. I soon discovered that Johnny and I had gotten into a synchronous rhythm in our picking up lint movement with neither person's head turning toward the other. After about ten minutes, I got up, exited the playroom, and crossed over the narrow hall to Dr. Kanner's office directly across. I sat in a chair facing Dr. Kanner with my back to the playroom. I was to report the history obtained from the parents to Dr. Kanner, looking fixedly at him as he looked fixedly at me. To my amazement, after five or so minutes, unseen by me, Johnny left the playroom, crossed the hall, passed by my chair and went over to Dr. Kanner's chair. With Dr. Kanner looking directly at me as I continued to talk, and Dr. Kanner giving no indication of his awareness of Johnny by his side, Johnny looked with what seemed like comfortable interest at the chair? At Dr. Kanner? Listening to our conversation. What I came to understand is that Dr. Kanner had us construct a situation in which Johnny was protected from a demand for intimacy in the form of face-to-face emotional and verbal interaction. Freed of the pressure to socialize and communicate to which he was totally turned off in his autistic shell, he could continue his interest in manipulating objects (picking up lint) and expand his interest to observing and exploring non-threatening non-demanding (human) objects. An additional factor may have been that my parallel lint picking may have been experienced by Johnny as sharing and supporting his interest. If so, Johnny would view me as a helper rather than a threat or hinderer.

A comment on terms

We use the term autism to designate the developmental problem of children described by Kanner and Asperger. We believe, as did Oliver Sacks (1995), that no two people with autism are the same in form or expression so that if we hope to understand the autistic individual a total biography is needed. The principal goal of Dr. Thielst and me is to help the reader understand the experience of Anna and Dr. T, of a daughter with autism and mutism and her mother. This requires two comparisons. One is to compare the experience of Anna with the experience of a well adapted neonate and one-year-old. The second comparison is between Anna's capacities and those of other neonates and infants on the autistic spectrum.

In referring to children or adults with autism, we have chosen to not follow the recommendation of those hoping to avoid the stigma often associated with individuals who have developmental disabilities or mental illness. Where we see her mother having helped Anna overcome debilitating symptoms of a maladaptive condition, they would see Anna and others as following a different developmental pathway, an example of neurodiversity. An analogy to diabetes will help to portray our view. Like autism, the negative impact on an individual's wellbeing emerges at different ages and has differing degrees of effect. Like autism, diabetes needs to be recognized (diagnosed) and treated as early as possible with differing degrees of intense interventions called for. Like autism, diabetes is a chronic condition, one that remains throughout life impacting emotional and physical functioning. We believe that tracking Anna and her mother's struggle with the maladaptive limitations of autism (like the maladaptive limitations of diabetes) – the successes and failures in amelioration – best tells the life story as it was and is being lived.

Another useful analogy is that when we think of someone having diabetes we recognize a condition that requires treatment but assume that he or she has many qualities and capacities that would facilitate living a productive satisfying life. We know that if untreated a person with diabetes can have serious emotional and cognitive disruptions from hypo- and hyperglycemia as well as other impairments, but the tilt in how the person is viewed is as a valued member of society. Unfortunately, for people with autism the tilt is opposite. Their limitations are emphasized – not their capacities. Even their frequently remarkable skills and determination, their systematizing inclinations, are pathologized rather than appreciated for their unique adaptive potential. Even when Anna had been mute, unresponsive to her name, and wildly reckless in her behavior, her mother recognized Anna's ability to play constructively with Lego and respond to music. Everyone else – family and professional – saw first a normally developing child, and then *only* pathology – deafness or worse – a candidate for an institution.

The analogy to how diabetes is viewed without stigma can serve as a model for autism. Without effective treatment, diabetes can make it impossible for a person to live a self-managed independent life. Even more so, without effective intervention, autism can make it impossible for many people to live a self-managed independent life. But fortunately, with the proper treatment, patients with diabetes and children with autism can work toward high degrees of self-management. As is now true of Anna who leads a rich independent life as a professional, Gus who at 14 could walk to school unaccompanied, and Owen who could write and give an explanatory lecture to a large audience about how Disney movie characters helped him find sidekicks, relate to people, and find love and joy. Ron Suskind, father of Owen, states the purpose of *Life Animated*:

> is driving a new way of thinking about how to reach kids like Owen by discovering their passions, what we call their 'affinity,' and turning it into a pathway for emotional, social, and cognitive growth. There are so many folks like Owen—those who are different and seen as less. They're not.
>
> (2014, p. 372)

The etiology of early infantile autism

No unified agreement exists as to the cause of early infantile autism. General belief points to a genetic disturbance or disorder. Many theoreticians and observers believe that additional sources – birth trauma, anoxia, chemicals, and toxic substances – operate as triggers that activate the onset. Piven, Elison, and Zylka state that research findings:

> suggest a conceptual framework for the early post-natal development of autism. This framework postulates that an increase in the proliferation of neural progenitor cells and hyper-expansion of cortical surface area in the first year, occurring during a pre-symptomatic period characterized by disrupted sensorimotor and attentional experience leads to altered experience-dependent neuronal development and decreased elimination of neuronal processes. This process is linked to brain volume overgrowth and disruption of the refinement of neural circuit connections.
>
> (2017, p. 1)

The authors state that the rate in which the proliferation and hyper-expansion takes place is more significant than the quantity.

Stated differently, first a pathological neuroanatomical disturbance takes place that interferes with sensory experiences (visual, auditory, and tactile) and relational interactions. Second, the absence of these usual formative experiences leads to crucial experience-dependent neuronal formation and neuro-connections failing to development. The sequence is: altered brain development results in the absence of formative lived experience. The deficit in formative lived experience results in a deficit in areas of brain development. The combination of a deficit in formative lived experience and a deficit in neural formation and connection results in the infant with autism turning off to and away from critical human interactions.

A different contribution to an understanding of the etiology of infantile autism derives from Narrative and Meaning (Lichtenberg, Lachmann, & Fosshage, 2017). The mini-narratives that give meaning to early inter subjective development (mother comes – smile – nice; or mother comes – frown – ugh) do not form as with Anna or are lost or inaccessible. These and other mini-narratives of being helped, soothed, regulated and being protected are the foundation of positive intersubjectivity, identity, and intimacy. Many children with autism, especially if non-verbal like Anna, need to borrow narrative and conversational skills from cartoon characters.

Once the autistic pattern is activated in the newborn, young infant or toddler, an understanding of the effects and outcome requires an interactive, intersubjective, and relational perspective. The interactive: a caregiver (mother, nanny) approaches a neonate or young infant expecting to hug, talk to, make eye contact, comfort, and feed, only to have the infant gives no indication of responsiveness, no alerting, no eye contact, no head turned toward but turned away, no calming response to holding, soothing, rocking.

The intersubjective effect: the infant forms no connection between whatever emotion or sensation he/she experiences, and the emotion being experienced by the caregiver. In turn, the caregiver, failing to get a response from her efforts to interact – facial expression, touch, talk – is confused, puzzled, disheartened, annoyed, painfully disappointed, and subject to self-blame, guilt, shame, and humiliation. The psychic field in which caregiver and infant coexist frequently takes on an increasingly negative ambiance. Often, the confused and ineffectual mother who may be blamed for the child's condition becomes increasingly despondent and feels guilty and the autistic infant withdraws into total aversive avoidance and retreats into a protective shell.

The relational perspective: the infant, toddler, or pre-school child and the primary caregiver and other caregivers form whatever patterns of interaction that allow them to coexist and minimize the limited communication, emotional disconnecting, erratic behavior, and oddity of gesture and tension reducing quirks of the child. Rather than seeking relational contact, the autistic child often prefers to be alone and left alone. Simultaneous with the child's interpersonal failure to relate, he or she will form highly invested interest in inanimate objects – Lego, blocks, numbers, machinery, time schedules, weather maps, cartoons.

Over the course of time, experience with the treatment and life patterns of autistic individuals has led to a different way to frame the question of etiology: is the neurobiological endowment for intimacy – sensing how others feel, reading facial expression, apprehending other's intentions, communicating with nuance, and playing imaginatively – *absent or present but, for some unknown reason, not activated*? When I regard the tremendous effort Dr. T and Anna made to activate Anna's sharing a connection with her mother and acquire language, I consider Anna's capacity for at least a level of intimacy and for communication skills to be present but needing a remarkably creative effort to turn on.

The problem of successfully activating is complex: first, the absence of turn on in the neonate or infancy period, second, the almost impenetrable avoidant shell built up against the intrusive demand for something – some response she can't give, and third, the disuse of the motor coordination needed for speech in those infants with mutism. Anna's activation came in two phases. The first phase was responding to her name, then the long interactive effort to sit with, to look at, to form categories, to discover what was meant by a question, to connect cross-modal vision, sound, touch, and body movement. A huge effort was required for her to switch onto the fundamentals of language – not yet communication – and minimal effort to activate knowledge of math.

The second phase was a sudden emotion-laden interaction with "others" – cartoon characters – in which Anna spontaneously took the lead to meet them.

> I remember the moment I opened it. I remember how I couldn't stop reading it. I memorized every single thing there, including the page number for each spoken phrase and how the faces of the characters looked like on each page. Knowing the volume of a book and a page

number enabled me to find quickly a particular happening or exchange of words between the characters whenever I wanted. I found it interesting how characters' faces changed while they were speaking to each other. I could see easily when they were angry or laughing while saying different things. My favorite place to go became that particular bookstore. I have always known that I learned language through these comic books where the text and pictures were complementing each other. I still love these characters and remember how they talked to each other. I was living a life together with them. They taught me language and how language is used by talking with others.

Two other experiences of children with autism

Gus: To Siri with Love: A Mother, Her Autistic Son, and the Kindness of Machines

In *To Siri with Love* (Newman, 2017), a book replete with charm and humor, Judith Newman describes the story of Gus, her son with autism, against a backdrop of Henry (Gus's normal twin) and their father, a retired opera singer with many characteristics of the autism spectrum. Gus has perfect pitch and from an early age was more responsive to music than words. He could identify hundreds of songs heard on his iPod from two or three notes. Often, if his mother asked him to do something he world ignore her but using his responsiveness to music, she discovered that if she sang the request he would do it. In addition, he was intensely interested in machinery, escalators, trains, buses, turtles, and anything related to weather. He would talk to anyone in his apartment building lobby and anyone on the street, asking them about where they were going. He would wander off seemingly without a plan. His mother was uncertain that he would be able to walk alone to his nearby school until he was 14. Consistently chattering about any of his many interests, he exhausted the patience of his mother who was delighted when he began his many, many conversations with Siri, Apple's virtual assistant. When frustrated, he would hold his ears and withdraw. When happy, he would hop. With a serious inability to sleep, he required physical closeness to his mother, sleeping in the same bed with her for years. He was fascinated by a woman's feet, meowing to a stranger if he thought she had pretty "feeties." Generally good natured, he did not make a clear distinction between inanimate objects and people, taking his iPod to the Apple store so it could be near its friends.

Owen: Life Animated: A Story of Sidekicks, Heroes, and Autism

Until about three, Owen had been a chatty, relating child (*Life Animated: A Story of Sidekicks, Heroes, and Autism*, Suskind, 2014). Then suddenly he became mute, cried inconsolably, and didn't sleep, eat or respond when spoken to. Unresponsive to others, Owen became totally tuned in to Disney movies. His parents and older brother discovered that if they assumed the identity and speech patterns of a Disney character, Owen would respond as another Disney character. Owen's interest expanded beyond the filmed interaction. He used the film's narratives to explore companionship – "sidekicks," and values and courage – heroes. Understanding the actions of heroes, with the help of his family he moved to a concept of the hero within. Owen was also able to draw his own versions of his cartoon side-kicks and a narrative about them that he created. All of this re-animation of Owen's life after the onset of autism was facilitated by his family's joining him in his responsiveness to Disney characters.

Interest and purpose: expanding the scope of being a doer doing

In *Uniquely Normal: Tapping the Reservoir of Normalcy to Treat Autism* (2017), Robert Bernstein and Cantor-Cooke describe 27 examples of young and older autistic individuals with whom they intervened therapeutically. Dr. Temple Grandin states that "The 27 case histories in this book cover the full range of the autism spectrum" (XIII).

Many similarities exist between the approaches and methods of Mr. Bernstein and Dr. Traugott. Dr. Thielst learned from Dr. Traugott that Anna would not attend or respond unless her interest was aroused and the activity – speech and/or behavior – seemed useful, that is, had a purpose that Anna could discern herself. In the rapid presenting and switching of cards with elephant and bird – using words, images, colors, sounds, and touch – Dr. Thielst captured Anna's interest. For Anna, the purpose was to add words as designators of images and objects to her existing systematized categories of Lego, trains, math, and music. The purpose for Dr. T was to build Anna's vocabulary so that Anna could read and from reading learn how people (first Disney characters and then her mother and others) converse and interact purposefully.

Mr. Bernstein and Cantor-Cooke emphasize seeking and building on the autistic individual's existing or spontaneously stimulated patterns of interest. For example, after other failures with Jeff, a non-verbal six-year-old who bit his hand until it bled to ease stress, he rolled a little toy car toward Jeff who rolled it back. Back and forth it went with Mr. Bernstein saying "Go, Go" each time. Then Mr. Bernstein held the car in a preparatory position – and held – and held – until to the total surprise of Jeff's gasping mother, Jeff said his first word Go. Jeff's interest was stimulated by the rolling car play. And now, as never before, his uttering a word had a use – a purpose – to continue the interrupted game.

In another example, Patrick, a severely autistic, non-verbal 11-year-old, was randomly picking up and putting down object after object in Mr. Bernstein's office as he babbled continuously. Mr. Bernstein observed that Patrick dropped a ball too big for his hand. Mr. Bernstein said "Where?" as the ball was searched for and found. Mr. Bernstein then gave Patrick different-sized cardboard blocks that Patrick arranged. When Patrick wasn't looking, Mr. Bernstein took a block. As Patrick noticed, Mr. Bernstein said "Where?" This opened the way to a hide-and-seek game in which the word "where" now had a purposeful meaning.

Dr. Thielst utilized a similar pattern in opening math to Anna. She established a grouping of paired receptacles with five objects in one and fewer in the other and a place for Anna to find, and retrieve, the missing number of objects. Knowing a quantity – two, three, and so on now had a purpose – to create a desired matching.

In each example, an interest of an autistic person – built on the foundation of an already formed pattern for systematizing – was used to activate a spontaneously stimulated interest that conveyed a use, a desirable purpose, a motivation.

In another example, Dr. T took Anna to a restaurant in which she would order Anna's favorite food time and time again. Then on one occasion she ordered something else not to Anna's liking. To everyone's surprise Anna said "No" and ordered for herself. The spoken word "No" – not the negating behavior – was now incorporated in Anna's repertoire of being a doer doing.

In *Enlivening the Self* (Lichtenberg, Lachmann, & Fosshage, 2016), we proposed that experiencing oneself as a doer doing, initiating and responding, activating and taking in is central to the core development and continuity of a sense of self. Interest as referred to here is a strong motivating emotion – one that transcends the psychic influence implied in its usual cognitive connotation. Interest, like anger, fear, joy, and love, activates an intention – to explore – and a goal – to master the skills needed to meet a challenge.

All of the children with autism to whom I have referred – Anna, Gus, Owen, Jeff, and Patrick were doers doing before the successful remedial efforts of the families and therapists. In their isolated states, they were organizers of blocks, babblers, and memorizers – all interests that allowed them to be initiators and responders, activators and taking in of self-learned skills. They were also doers doing in respect to bodily needs. What they weren't was doers doing in respect to human relatedness – neither by interest nor by sense of purpose. Jeff's saying "Go" was to activate Dr. Bernstein so Jeff could continue his interest in the game – speech now had a purpose. Anna's saying "No" and ordering her favored food was to activate her mother and the waitress so she could enjoy her preferred meal – particular foods being a long-held interest of hers. In each instance, initiating through words was used to ensure an already activated interest in obtaining an inanimate goal (play or food) but gave a newly discovered purpose to conversation with a human other.

As Mr. Bernstein describes, Anna, Jeff, and Patrick had each tapped into their:

> reservoir of normalcy. Anyone who knows a child with autism well knows what this looks like. It may be a facial expression or gesture or an action. It may happen only rarely, but it happens, and in that moment the child is thinking, feeling and processing typically.
>
> (p. 84)

The key is to recognize the stir of interest and follow its path for a sense of purpose to emerge.

Chapter 6

At birth what becomes activated in normal development and fails to become activated in neonates with autism

What capacities do full-term healthy neonates bring that enables the emergence of their adaptive development along the three major pathways to 1) Human relatedness and intimacy, 2) a healthy functioning body and mind–body connection, and 3) mastery of the environment? By adaptive development I mean becoming a feeling, sensing doer doing, initiating and responding, activating and taking in, modeling and innovating in a context of receptive caregivers. *What capacities of a neonate evidencing autism are absent or at such variance that adaptive development does not go forward?*

1 The ability to seek and respond affectively to a variety of stimuli

   1a Responding to affectively pleasing interactions with caregivers and others to establish a category of wanting and seeking warm relationships that in time (along with smiling and sensual enjoyment) becomes encoded as a loving intimacy. *In autistic infants like Anna this response pattern is not activated at birth. With Owen it was only to disappear just before his third birthday.*

   1b Responding to affectively unpleasant, noxious, painful interactions through the establishment of a category of aversiveness and antagonism, rage and hatred or avoidance, fear, and disdain. *The response pattern leading to intimacy becomes rigidly and painfully aversive leading to a psychic wall of avoidance.*

   1c Responding to stimuli too high in intensity or too great a breach of expectation with confusion and withdrawal. Responding to repetitions of stimuli too low in activating interest with apathy and failure to thrive. *In autism, the response pattern of facial contact is experienced as too high in intensity and too confusing about what emotional interaction is called for. In contrast, interaction with inanimate objects – Lego, machinery, maps – and other symbolic systems – math, music – may be richly activating.*

2 From their experience in the intrauterine environment neonates bring a differentiated recognition of their mother's voice, a pattern of sucking to self-soothe, and body movements to move away from noxious stimulation. *For infants with autism the activation is split: self-soothing (Anna's rhythmical rocking) and aversive withdrawal are activated, the seeking response to mother's voice is not.*

3 Responsiveness to a human face, preferentially to the eyes and mouth areas. *Aversive and avoided.*

4 Having a 10–12-inch visual focal point that concentrates gaze, attention, and interest on the sphere of mother infant feeding, holding, and social interchange and then gradually expands with a comparable expansion of interest to the broader environment. *In autism the gaze is differentially directed away from the caregiver's face and toward objects in the environment.*

5 Responding to smell with a heightened sensitivity to mother's smell that along with vision, auditory, and kinesthetic interactions contributes to a strong discriminating recognition of the primary caregiver. *Not activated.*

6 Responding positively to the human voice with a heightened reactivity to higher pitch and especially to prosody and musicality. *In Dr. T's working with Anna, the responsiveness to higher pitch and musicality went on to become an important feature but not integrated with facial communication. Gus was strongly turned on to music from an early age.*

7 Having exquisite sensitivity to temporal features in the environment – beat, duration, and rhythm. *Present outside of human interaction.*

8 Via the rooting reflex, to seeking and responding to a nipple with sucking to reduce hunger sensation and experience fullness and relief. *Sucking to reduce hunger will be activated, but in infants with autism it may or may not (as with Anna) be to the mother's nipple. When it is, the experience will not be toward the usual full relationship. Feeding often will not take the form of close cuddling but will be more mechanical. Gus needed close proximity to his mother's body to sleep.*

9 Readily initiating a high percentage of interactions with a caregiver. These frequent initiatives (Winnicott's spontaneous gestures) give the caregiver an opportunity to recognize, affirm, and validate the infant's budding agency, his/her affects, intention, and goals. For the infant, this experience coheres into a sense of self as a doer doing with others. *Rather than with a caregiver, most interactions are activated with an inanimate object.*

10 When distressed and disrupted, responding to comforting with the restoration of a calm state and a return of the ability to activate interest. *Children with autism are generally difficult, even resistant to comforting, preferring to be left alone to reduce tension through body movements like rocking, twitching, hopping, and an intent repetitive focus on manipulating objects.*

11 Imitating and mimicking observed movements and gestures. *No affect sharing, initiating and modeling of human interactional patterns, but movements organized to manipulate objects.*

12 Active readiness to recognize, respond to and be affected by the emotions of caregivers. *Least activated. Infants with autism have a serious inability to integrate the emotions they experience with the emotional experience of those around them.*

13 Actively scanning for and responding with interest to changes in the environment – such as light, touch, and movement. *Often activated, sometimes strongly in particular areas like weather changes and escalators with Gus and vehicles and piano keys with Anna.*

14 Responding to repetitions of events – such as caregiver's face approaching and receding by developing a sense of familiarity that then becomes categorized and remembered with an affective tonality. *Not activated.*

15 Recognizing the contrast between a novel stimulus and recurrent familiar experience and establishing a new category. *Activated in the non-human environment.*

16 Responding to a stimulus presented in one or more sensory modes both in that mode and in alternate (cross) modes as well – visual, auditory, taste, smell, touch, gesture, motor action. *Blocked off in human interaction. Present otherwise.*

17 Having a largely unrestricted pathway from body sensations of all types to psychic affective arousal that gradually becomes more

regulated so that body sensations become less dominant factors in ordinary consciousness. *In children with autism, regulation of physiological requirements may be more or less difficult but is able to be activated. Sensory hypersensitivities are common.*

18 Recognizing contingencies guided by innate biases and affectively charged values especially the contingencies that involve helpful or hindering responses to the neonate's intentions and goals. *Helpfulness in dealing with desires activated in mastery of the nonhuman environment may be recognized and appreciated, less so with need involving attachment.*

19 A capacity to rapidly build expectations from any repeated category of experience. *Children with autism rapidly build negative expectations about human interchange and positive expectations about solitary play with objects.*

Comparing adaptive qualities and capacities normally emerging in the first year of life with the more limited resources of the one-year-old infant with autism

From an extensive review of observation and research, Lichtenberg, Lachmann, and Fosshage (2016) identified 12 qualities and capacities that emerge in the first year of life. When present, these qualities and capacities provide the major steps on the pathway to the development of an enlivened sense of self capable of forming healthy intimate relationships, bodily health, mastery of the environment, and an excellent prospect of success in meeting subsequent life challenges. I will present and describe the 12 qualities and capacities and a brief summary of the origins of their development. *I will then describe the presence or absence of the qualities and capacities in children with autism.*

An important caveat: children within the autistic and Asperger spectrum vary greatly in time of onset and the degree of positive and/or limited development at every age. For example, Anna as a neonate began life aversive to emotional interplay with her mother while the turning off from emotional contact and overstimulation occurs later for Gus and other autistic spectrum infants and toddlers. Anna babbled disconnected word-like approximations until the age of five while many infants with autism are verbal.

By the end of their first year well adapted children will have:

1 *Established a healthy balance for receptivity and activation of positive and negative affective experience.* A parent's happy smile elicits a reciprocal response of a happy smile from a three-month-old infant (Sanders, 1983; Lichtenberg, Lachmann, & Fosshage, 2016). An eager readiness on both their parts sets the stage for their next exchange of joy. Conversely, an infant with a depressed mother will be drawn in by her mood. Her depression will likely deepen as a result of the infant's negative responsiveness. The dystonic emotions of both will become more fixed by the emergent negative ambiance they co-create (Tronick, 2002). With each subsequent life event, the threshold level for activating a positive or negative affect might be reinforced or modified (Tronick & Cohn, 1989). In everyday life, good experiences – conscious and/or unconscious – will reinforce a prior low threshold (easy receptivity) for positive emotions. If repeated, good experiences gradually modify a higher threshold, lowering the barrier to receptivity so that positive emotion can be more readily experienced. In addition, positive experiences can raise the threshold (lessen the receptivity) for negative emotions so that they not as readily experienced.

   For the one-year-old infant with autism, the balance between receptivity and activation of positive and negative affective experience does not derive from fluctuation of joyous and troubled interactions with caregivers. An infant with autism commonly experiences face-to-face interactions as confusing, overwhelming, and aversive. Positive emotional experience occurs in feeding, while manipulating objects, and being left alone – that is not appealed to for an emotional response to a relational interaction.

2 *Developed explicit and implicit confidence that disruptions in relationships and pursuits will be repaired and a more optimal context restored.* Repetitive experiences of caregiver–infant success in repairing disruptions and restoring an optimal context for each to be a doer with the other establishes an implicit expectation that setbacks can be mastered with confidence. Similarly, repetitive experiences of infant–caregiver's failures to repair disruptions establish a fear and dread that they cannot be mastered with confidence (Kohut, 1984). Failure to respond to a child's physical or severe emotional distress, especially if

prolonged or repetitive, erodes confidence in the effectiveness of the reparative effort of others and of the child (Beebe & Lachmann, 2002).

Sadly, an infant with autism like Anna not only develops no confidence in the effectiveness of others to repair disruptions but often experiences greater disruptions from the efforts of caregivers to comfort. Confused by and aversive to the caregiver's efforts and emotion, infants with autism rely on their own efforts through rocking like Anna or twitching, spinning, walking on tippy-toes and other body movements to self-soothe.

3 *Formed a sense that one's self and others have a positive identity based on affirming attributions.* Parents continuously form attributions about their children and about themselves as parents, often beginning even before the children are born. As soon as their capacity for verbal symbolism emerges, infants give word labels (good boy, good mommy, bad boy, mean mommy) to their prior and current encoded imagistic memory experiences. An attribution might be limited to how one's self and others are seen to be in specific areas of endeavor, or it might become a more generalized identity characterization of the self and the other.

In the first year of life of an infant with autism, the infant and his or her parents live in an emergent atmosphere of puzzled dismay – neither knowing how to react to and with the other. In such an atmosphere the parents' attribution about their child is apt to be critical and shaming – he hates me, she must be dumb or deaf, she is nasty like her father's family. On the other side, the child with autism's negative attribution about the parents will generally not be a verbal reference but a full body turn off and aversion.

4 *Experienced a sense of being known and fully recognized for one's authentic qualities, capacities, and sensibilities.* Closely tied to the power of attributions derived from prior lived experience is the child's sense of being known. When a child has been mirrored across a range of affects, intentions, goals, and especially modes of responsive relating, the child can place itself more securely in the world with what Winnicott (1960, p. 46) called a "true self." Frequently, the child's own deep sense of authenticity exerts a positive influence on the responses of others. Alternatively, when the child's inherent emergent capacities have been ignored, rejected, misidentified, the child is often forced to adopt a false self via pathological accommodation (Brandchaft, Doctors, & Sorter, 2010).

Typically, an infant with autism is known for what she or he isn't – a joy giving relating little one rather than the person she or he is – a potential contributor – puzzlingly peculiar, often wildly undisciplined – but a valuable human being – and sometimes like Anna one who is uniquely gifted. For the child with autism, any capacity to know her or himself can be so delayed and so dependent on difficult heroic reparative effort as with Anna that too often the child, adolescent and grown-up individual with autism may never arrive at an authentic sense of self, an identity compatible with her or his potential. Like Anna, with the understanding and help they received Gus and Owen were able to use their special affinities for mastery of their environment to develop adaptive productive lives.

5   *The ability to predict their own initiatives and responses as well as those of others.* An infant's capacity to predict his or her patterns of initiating and responding can be observed in proto-conversations, and in a widening range of intentions and interactions (Stern, 1985; Beebe & Lachmann, 2002). A child's full sense of knowing itself can only be achieved if, as they develop, they are able to integrate their initiatives and responses with those of others – an integrated dual contingency.

The ability of infants with autism to predict initiatives and responses is uniquely two sided. On one side they have adaptive patterns that are sufficiently consistent for them to predict their intention and receptivity to being fed, and to the activation of their interest in manipulating objects and attending to some visual and non-human auditory stimuli. On the other side, their consistent aversion to face-to-face interaction and the communication of strong aversive emotional intentions that derive from it allows infants with autism to predict and anticipate their turn off responses.

6   *A capacity to form and share narratives.* Narratives are essential organizers of experience (Lichtenberg, Lachmann, & Fosshage, 2017). The human mind forms narratives from the continuous flow of body sensations and perceptual input, while awake, drowsing, or asleep, and no matter whether the individual is focused on a task, meditating, or engaged in mind wandering. Narratives are first formed in imagistic and action (gestural) sequences, then in scripts, and later as verbal depictions of increasing complexity. Narratives are essential for an autobiographic sense of self based on temporality, i.e., past, present, and future. One might say that the fullness

of our humanity derives from an ability to create stories, dramatize them in a theater of the mind, and then live more or less comfortably in the stories we create about ourselves, others, ourselves with others, and about the world we live in.

Children with autism will create sensation stories – tummy hurts, hungry, nose stopped up, bladder full – with or often without words. They will create stories based on vision – the light moving across the crib bars, sound – music, touch – the feel of a blanket. They will create stories of what interest them – the objects they like to manipulate or look at – or hear – or form, often with a heightened creative acuity. Stories critical for intimacy and relatedness – mother comes, calls my name, smiles; mother comes, frown, ugh – with the prosody of her voice, her affect and my response to it – are not created by those infants with early onset autism.

7 *Learned, understood, and internalized social norms.* Learning, understanding, and internalizing social norms are all early forms of adaptation required for children to become social beings. At three months, infants form narratives centering on moral and ethical values, and by three years, they appreciate and enforce the rules of games (Lichtenberg, Lachmann, & Fosshage, 2016, p. 66). Knowing social norms enhances the active child's sense of being able to predict their intentions and those of others, and provides confidence in being in the world. By contrast, when the social "norm" for an infant is to be raised in a family in which abuse regularly occurs, or in a neighborhood that is lawless and centered on drugs and violence, the child and later adult's "norm" will test the resources for adaptive behavior. When the infant's world is troubled in less destructive ways, school and peer activity presents a new field of social norms and a means to creatively modify maladaptive reactions to social expectations (Lichtenberg, Lachmann, & Fosshage, 2016, p. 67).

The inability to socialize, often evidenced by "wild behavior," as with Anna, is a critical problem for children with autism and for their parents. The absence of face-to-face communication limits the recognition of the affect and intention of others, and the mirroring and modeling of behavior that emerges from it. Consequently, an infant with autism lacks the guidance of cues needed to choose between acceptable and unacceptable behaviors. A one-year-old child with autism will distinguish between a helper and a hinderer but only as to his limited area of intentions and interests. The reciprocity for being helped by being a helper is seriously underdeveloped.

8 *Shared many moments of enlivened lived experience.* Sharing moments of enlivened experience, momentary or extended, produces a sense of commonality and safety. From the mirror-neuron activation of shared moments of mother and baby extruding their tongues to the shared smile on greeting to the later sharing of humor, an ironic perspective, an aesthetic sensibility – seeing eye-to-eye – when present invigorates all relationships (Lichtenberg, Lachmann, & Fosshage, 2016, p. 67).

Shared moments of the enlivened experience of intimacy are tragically lacking for a child with autism. Such moments of pleasurable achievement as he can fashion are his, not generally shared. The absence of shared enlivened moments has an adverse effect, a severe disappointment, on a parent, and contributes to further isolation for the infant.

9 *Be able to play with others, play when alone and evoke a sense of another, and generate a spirit of playfulness.* A mother playing with her responsive baby, with their eyes widening, tongues extruding, hands moving, eyes brightening at first in response to their mother's approach, then smiling and giggling, breathes life into movement in a shared world of joy and playfulness. The evolutionary preparedness of the new-born is demonstrated by how rapidly – after a mother has initiated a playful interaction – the infant takes further initiative if the other does not. It has been said that play is a serious business, and indeed it is. Once well established in the intersubjective realm of the infant in the first year, play provides a foundation, an underlying hum, for many aspects of learning, mastery, sensual and sexual sharing, and creativity (Lichtenberg, Lachmann, & Fosshage, 2016, pp. 67–68).

Play with a child with autism is often solitary, repetitive, obsessive, and joyless. In addition, these children have a severe lack or restriction of mind play and creative fantasy involving loving others, buddies, and sidekicks.

10 *Experienced other and self through physical touch and later the metaphor of feeling touched by another.* Lived experiences involving physical and metaphoric touch help to integrate body and mind (Beebe et al., 2010). Touch is a significant mode of agency in the development and regulation of a sense of self. Self or caregiver touch provides a means of soothing, of playful arousal, and sets a sensual

tonality to acting both by oneself and with another. Self-touch and being touched embodies physiological, attachment, caregiving, exploratory, and sensual/sexual experiences (Lichtenberg, 1989, 2008). The reciprocity involved in feeling touched emotionally by the other is a fundamental basis of physical and conceptual intimacy (Lichtenberg, Lachmann, & Fosshage, 2016, p.67).

Children with autism often withdraw from the touch of others as a component of face-to-face and other communication. They are left to rely on self-touch, rocking, spinning, twitching, hopping, and running about often wildly to release tension.

11 *Learned to cooperate in spirit and interaction.* Infant and caregiver cooperation is a fundamental basis of reciprocity in all of an infant's activities with others. Cooperation results from the ability of each to recognize and respond to the initiatives of the other, and cannot develop if an infant's initiatives are ignored or overwhelmed. Cooperation involves negotiating the polarities of compliance and opposition. Empathy, sensing the state of mind and intentions of the other, develops in parallel with cooperation (Lichtenberg, Lachmann, & Fosshage, 2011). In *The Primary Triangle*, Fivaz-Depeursinge and Corboz-Warnery (1999) study a family triad of mother, father, and infant attempting a series of tasks: one parent playing with the infant, the other parent playing with the infant, all three playing together and mother and father with each other. The research indicates that some triads cooperate easily and well. Other triads can overcome an obstacle one member introduces. In another triad, the tendency of one pair to collude with each other and leave out the third precludes cooperation. Other triads function so chaotically that even a semblance of cooperation fails to occur.

Children with autism not only lack patterns of cooperation but little conception of its meaning and spirit. Not only do they frustrate caregivers who attempt to get them to cooperate but their puzzling and aversive behavior often creates problems that destroy the cooperative spirit not only with them but between their parents and extended family members as with Dr. T and her family. Rather than cooperation, blaming, guilt, and shame may become dominant in family life.

12 *Experienced many heightened affect moments of surprise, awe, and admiration.* A parent's surprise, awe, and admiration in regard to some "wonderful" action of their infant and an infant's wide-eyed

acknowledgement of something "wonderful" their parent has just done facilitate the emergence of a special quality of invigoration, that can, then, be experienced as "magic" moments throughout life. A wondrous sunset, a trapeze artist's brilliance, and the "aha" moment of a sudden insight, to be shared with a responsive other, are moments in everyday life that enliven the human spirit. Alternatively, surprise, awe, and admiration can be exploited by parents, siblings, teachers, and cult leaders to inspire fear and dread, to make themselves feel powerful and magically brilliant and to leave the child or individual feeling small, weak, and dependent.

Sadly, children with autism miss out on sharing with the caregiver moments of feeling my mom, my dad, my sister knows just what I want and how I feel – I think she is great and I share in that good feeling. Alternatively, skills with inanimate objects or with math, music, drawing or other symbol systems – sometimes remarkable as with Anna, Gus, and Owen – possessed by children with autism can lead to an experience of surprise, awe, and admiration.

Chapter 7

A doer doing and the core sense of self

We (Lichtenberg, Lachmann, & Fosshage, 2016, 2017) have proposed that an infant's core sense of self develops in conjunction with the experience of being a doer doing across a spectrum of repetitive activities with a caregiver or alone – feeding, awakening, being picked up, carried, put down, crying, watching changes in lights and shadows while lying in the crib. Each experience of the doer doing – his/her affects, intentions, and goals – is synthesized into a mini-story organized along hedonic lines – feels good/feels bad; sensually pleasurable/aches/and hurts; helpful/hindering. Some interactions and responses of a doer doing are organized to function rapidly and largely non-consciously as action/interaction procedures such as grasping for a presented toy or thumb sucking when distressed. Some operate consciously as attempts to gain mother's attention or to choose a particular doll. Procedural intentions such as grasping and thumb sucking, and conscious intentions such as appealing to mother for her attention or selecting a favored doll from a group emerge as sensorimotor stories (narratives) of I want. Other groupings of affects, intentions, and goals become integrated into sensorimotor stories of I don't want – I turn my head away, I spit out, I bang my hand, I push it away, I scream NO.

While many experiences of a doer doing occur when alone, those that involve interacting with a caregiver are fundamental to all later intimate relationships. In many of these interactions the caregiver is the initiator and activator and the infant the responder and taker in. At other times, the infant is the initiator and activator, the caregiver the responder and taker in. In the continued reciprocity of these interactions, the infant will get to know (recognize) his/her mother – her affects and intentions, and his/her responses to her. In turn, she will take in the experience of her infant and get to know (recognize) the doer doing he/she has become, is, and from prediction who he/she will be. Central to the infant's success as a doer doing is his/her ability to pick up cues to guide his/her implicit and explicit choices during their reciprocal interactions. The intimate reciprocal interactions of mother and baby are not orderly turn-taking initiation and responding. Each next step in intimate relational interactions is co-created, negotiated as joint intentions and directions between partners on a moment-to-moment basis. Cues inform each partner not only what is explicitly stated as information or intention, but also an implicit indication of the meaning of the relationship as a dyad – a "we" as well as you and I.

Infant–mother face-to-face interactions and the development of conversational language

In face-to-face conversational interactions infants look intently at their mother's face – especially eyes and mouth. Why? To engage – yes. But also to infer mother's emotions and intentions. The infant is picking up on subtle fleeting cues that orient him/her to be an effective engaging doer doing. From infancy on the inclination to read cues – register intentions and emotions – verbal or especially non-verbal – is so basic it often seems automatic. To explain how each partner in the dyad lets each other know about their inner feeling state, Stern (1985) proposes affect attunement, a form of selective and cross-modal imitation. Preverbal infants and mothers precisely time the starting, stopping and pausing of their vocalizations to create a rhythmic coupling and bi-directional coordination of their vocal dialogues. From all these subtle interactional cues, infant and mother intuit each other's intentions and emotions. The infant doer doing absorbs and learns language as an emergent accompaniment to an implicit appreciation of his/her and mother's emotions and intentions. Acquiring language as an emergent aspect of face-to-face conversational interaction adds definition to the already formed enrichment of gestural, imagistic, and sensation narratives. Conversational language emerges as an integral aspect of affect-laden mother–baby face-to-face communication. The affect, its vitality, timbre, and prosody, gives conversational language and the intentions and goals it conveys its meaning.

The distinction between learning words as designators and language as a means to converse with others and one's self is beautifully illustrated in the narrative of Dr. T and Anna. As a consequence of the failure of their initial relationship, Anna had neither the ability to converse or words as designators. Other children with autism may acquire a vocabulary but their conversation is stilted and without the flow of affect and prosody that conveys personal meaning – the subtle shades of feeling that demonstrate and build intimacy. Dr. T's creative tutelage, based on Dr. Traugott's direction, enabled Anna to read so she could acquire systematically basic vocabulary words as designators and to use them in phrases and sentences to make choices as with food in the store. The words and an ability to read gave her a degree of mastery of her environment but not the ability to converse. She turned on to conversation in a sudden burst of recognition derived from an emotional entry into a scene of interacting Disney characters. She felt safe. She was free of the bewildering overwhelming overstimulating puzzle of human faces – full of emotion – trying to involve and direct her. Donald Duck – his face and the emotion on it – was fixed. The bubble of words was now readable. What Donald said was intelligible and clearly meant to convey an intention to Mickey Mouse. And then a compelling back and forth emerged between them – a conversation. Anna got it on her own and from then on it was hers.

Disney's animated movies provided a similar opportunity for Owen to appreciate affective conversations and the meanings inherent in many interactions and for his family to find a way to communicate with him. For Gus, the animated figures were people coming in and out of the resident building where he played substitute doorman, strangers on the street whom he greeted with a ritual patter, and Siri with which he carried on lively conversations about his areas of deep interest. Viewing the figures in a comic book cartoon or an animated movie with the flattening of their facial expression or conversing back and forth with a passing parade of strangers or a computerized voice allows a child with autism to learn from safely distant characters who can tell him what they are up to – their affects, intentions, and goals. And can use them both to learn from about interaction and to be his imaginary sidekicks. In contrast, a child with autism viewing an argument between his parents will sense something is happening that involves angry affects and hostile intentions similar to those he has felt. But the whole experience will likely be so overwhelming and confusing that rather than appreciating what the content is and what position each is taking, he will likely hold his ears, race about, or escape to his room.

What experience is lost to the autistic infant's avoidance of face-to-face, eye-to-eye communication? I propose that in the course of the usual comfortable infant/mother face-to-face communication and many other caregiver activities, the infant synthesizes and integrates the essential core of a capacity for intimacy: the ability to intuit the emotions and intentions of the other as they impact the self; the ability to read subtle cues that guide the infant's responses to emotions and intentions of the mother; the forming of a narrative about who mother is with him/her and some idea of what she wants from him/her; the ability to recognize conversational cues of start, stop, pause, wait, and go that later words, sentences, and prosody rich language seamlessly fit into. And expanding from the infant/mother communication, categories of similar intimate interactions leading to intuiting the emotions and intentions of other familiar people – especially father, siblings, and pets.

Faces – the pathway to intimacy; inanimate objects – the pathway to mastery

Research and observation demonstrate that by the end of the first year healthy infants have acquired from their face-to-face interactions with a caregiver an integrated package or gestalt of:

1   Knowing how to read cues about the effects and intentions of others, the affects and intentions of themselves as a doer doing and the reciprocal interplay of dyadic affects and intentions – the foundation for empathy, mentalization, and a theory of mind.
2   The cues of how to carry on a conversation – first non-verbal, later verbal with all the subtlety of stops, pauses, and starts coordinated with the affect-laden prosody and musicality of speech.
3   The beginning affect-laden narrative of identity, who the infant is in the mirror of the caregiver, who the caregiver is in the interaction with the infant, and what affective ambiance they create between them – the emotional vitality of their intimacy – the foundation for creating imaginative characters and dramas in mind wandering and play sequences.
4   Patterns of behavior based on each's attentiveness to the intentions and goals of the other, coordinated with the caregiver's guiding the infant's intentions through mirroring, approval, and redirection – thereby providing the foundation of the infant doer's socialization.

From an aggregate of these developmental experiences emerges a child's or adult's capacity for intimacy: 1) knowing the interplay between the emotions and intentions of others and his or her own, 2) being able to converse through affectively rich subtle verbal and nonverbal means,

3) having a creatively rich imagination, and 4) being able to socialize with an expanding range of contacts. The pathway that is the foundation for intimacy differs from the integration that forms the foundation for the mastery of the environment. The pathway to the development of intimacy, conversation, imaginative interpersonal play, and socialization begins with recognition of and responsiveness to the human face and the musicality of the human voice. The pathway to the development of mastery of the environment begins with the recognition of an object, a thing (Lego, numbers, maps, machinery). Face recognition and object recognition occur in differing areas of the brain (the fusiform gyrus for the face, the interior temporal gyrus for the object (Schultz et al., 2000; Klin et al., 2003). Cartoons in comic books (Anna) and movies (Owen) are objects telling stories about people, their faces, and their conversations. For Gus, with his hyper responsiveness to music, his mother's singing rather than speaking her requests and Siri's answering his questions were object-people with whom he could interact as Anna would with Lego.

This distinction – separate areas of response to people and to objects in adaptive development and the same area of processing for both people and things in infants and adults with autism – leads to differences in how each view conversations with other humans – literally where they direct their visual focus. The person with autism directs his or her eyes away from the eyes of a speaker, sometimes looking at the mouth, sometimes at the shoulder, or just in the general area of the speaker (Klin et al., 2002). The result is the person with autism can and generally does learn the behavior necessary to participate in a conversational interaction but generally lacks recognition of the subtle or not-so-subtle nuances of meaning being communicated. Children and adults on the spectrum find it particularly difficult to distinguish between fully intentional emotional communication and implicitly expressed sub-themes and unintended meanings. They are often either unaware of or confused by reactions of others to their social awkwardness and tension releasing behaviors.

If we conceptualize children with autism viewing people as things, a goal might be for them to come to regard them as safe, interesting, potentially useful people-things rather than frightening overstimulating emotional face-things to get away from. We can regard Dr. T's enormous effort with Anna as having made this conversion from scary object-people to interesting object-people. Interesting to Anna like Lego, like math, like libraries, like object-people to sit next to in classes, like object-people to dance with. Owen could interact with his family and therapist when they adopted the persona of his favorite Disney characters and Gus with strangers on the street and Siri.

For an infant an object, say a rattle, plays a different role in her emotional state than a face. An infant doesn't want to get into her infant seat and begins to fuss and thrash about. Her mother tries to comfort her with no effect. Then as mother shakes a rattle before her eyes, the infant focuses on the rattle and its sound and instantly calms – a complete shift in her mental state – in her affect, intention, and goal. The infant's mother's effort to force her into the infant seat resulted in a disruption of their attachment experience and a shift into an aversive state. What did the rattle do? The rattle captured the infant's interest – interest being an affect state that when fully activated can fully capture the entire focus of the sense of self. The infant's goal shifts from an "I don't want to" to a let me look, hear, examine, make sense of, and play with. In a wonderful example of a shift from an aversive state to the calming of an arousal of interest, Dr. T describes that after Anna was fully turned on to solving math problems and before she could tolerate human interaction without serious aversion, Dr. T regularly carried a math practice book to instantly give to Anna when she saw the indication of Anna's upset. Book in hand, Anna immediately went to work, her interest aroused, her focus on solving the problem and implicitly increasing her skill and mastery building her confidence. Aversion to interactions in the interpersonal world with all the negative feelings that for Anna went with it was instantly transformed to an activation of interest, an urge toward efficacy, the building of confidence and all the enhancement of the sense of the self that emerges in the doer doing. This helps to explain how Anna, Gus, Owen, and many others with the interpersonal limitations inherent in autism develop such remarkable skills in the nonhuman challenges when given the opportunity.

A particularly important developmental advance is toward the complexity of functioning and enlivening of the sense of self that emerges from the interplay of existing lower-level subcortical and cortical functioning and the maturation of higher level cortical capacities. This change brings about reflective functioning and the diversity of more ordered narratives – played out with blocks and Lego, math problems, music skills, and borrowed from cartoons and books. Dr. T discovered that during the period before St. Petersburg when Anna did not speak, she had catalogued the number of trams in their native city and was amazed by the larger number in St. Petersburg.

An additionally surprising example of 10 to 20-month-old Anna's latent capacities was her remarkable ability to categorize her experience with inanimate objects evidenced by her early memories of their first house being next to a grocery store and the new house having an unfinished bathroom with a sign saying "1988" on the wall. In the new house she remembered details of the setting but more interesting was her memory of a male guest "who was smiling all the time and who gave me pink bunny slippers." Here is a breakthrough of early human relatedness propelled by "his extraordinary big smile" capturing her attention. I would add being so reassuringly consistent and benign that three-year-old Anna could read his face as sensually pleasing along with " the softness of the slippers and how they felt and looked and how the bunny ears were moving when I was running around." Anna ends this memory stating "I don't remember his wife." My speculation is that this was a three to four-year-old's breakthrough of an oedipal attachment moment – an experience much needed by Anna as a foundation for her later current romantic attachment. Considering these memories of her first four years confirms the belief that even when her autistic pattern was at its height, moments of physic organization of systemized categorizing and sensuality formed a resource available for her to build on later.

In contrast to their affinity for systematizing inanimate objects, children with autism are less inclined toward more imaginative narratives – make believe, hide and seek, Santa Claus, and ghosts under the bed. While the creation of the realm of fantasy and make believe derives from the intersubjective lived experience of adaptive development, children with autism whose more intense experience is with objects, conflate experience with animate and inanimate "objects." Gus's "relationship" with Siri and taking his iPod to the Apple store so it would be with friends are examples.

The pathway to a healthy body, physical functioning, and mind–body connection

From face-to-face conversational interchanges with caregivers, infants derive the cues needed to recognize the interplay of their and the caregiver's affects and intentions and the timing, rhythm, and musicality of verbal exchanges – the foundation of intimacy. From exposure to the interactional surround, infants derive the cues that call them to act: the movements of light and shadow are to watch, a ball is to throw, a piece of Lego is to attach to another piece, a teddy bear is to hold, a top is to spin, a toy truck is to push – the foundation of mastery of the environment. From the coordination between a body sensation that signals a physiological need and the caregiver's response, infants get the cues they need to signal to others and themselves about hunger, thirst, a stuffed-up nose, sleep, urination, defecation, needing exercise or rest, having discomfort or pain, as well as a general sense of bodily wellbeing or a dystonic state. Since messages in the form of sensation are continuously flowing between body and mind, each infant, child, and adult must learn which signal to attend and act on, and which to ignore or suppress without negative consequences – the foundation of physiological regulation and physical wellbeing.

For children with autism, the cues for relations with others that lead to empathy and intimacy are seriously underdeveloped. In contrast, the cues that lead to productive responses to the challenges of the inanimate world are often well developed. In this realm, these children are drawn to repetitions that lead to increasing efficacy. The confidence that emerges from mastery is a sustaining experience for many children and adults with autism. Anna, Gus, and Owen are talented individuals whose response to inanimate stimuli led to enriching experiences of mastery.

What about the cues for self-regulation that arise from the coordination between body sensation signals and caregiver efforts to regulate and protect their child's wellbeing? Dr. T indicates that Anna did well with physiological regulation in her own uncoordinated with mother way. As a small infant she would grab a bottle and suck vigorously. Later, she would go to the refrigerator to get her own food rather than be helped, touched, or have to speak or answer. She was fully potty trained and preferred to dress herself. Comforting by others was rejected. Self-soothing was accomplished by rocking from side to side. Taken for swimming lessons, Anna no longer refused to be held by her mother, but at moments she became so frightened that she clung to her mother's body as though it were a pillar.

Looked at overall, Anna, Gus, and Owen each had more or less knowledge of their own body sensations and regulatory cues learned from caregivers to have a sense of physical wellbeing. Gus was slow in growth, especially in comparison to his twin brother and growth hormones were considered. Common to autistic children is tension release through motor activity – rocking, hopping, twitching. Also common are sensory hypersensitivities – clothes feeling too tight or too rough, touch often being painful, while pressing tight against a firm surface may be soothing. Anna preferred to rock herself to sleep by herself. Gus couldn't sleep unless in bed with his mother, and Owen at the time of onset of autism couldn't sleep or eat and raced about wildly. In summary, with some exceptions, the developmental pathway to physical health and an effective connection between body and mind is generally adequate in people with autism.

Appearance, how one is seen and regarded, is an important factor in how a child, adolescent, or adult's physicality is experienced. Unfortunately, many children with autism are seen by their peers and by adults as odd, different. They may draw negative attention to themselves by avoiding looking at the other's face, not responding to an emotional signal, erratic wild behavior, idiosyncratic rocking, walking on tip toes, hopping, or jumping, and a general awkwardness in conversation and social responses. If they are laughed at, ridiculed, or mocked, they often do not recognize the reason for the negative response. How being seen as awkward, odd, and/or different varies in the negative effect on the autistic person. Anna was helped a great deal by her mother to manage better socially by such means as baking cookies for Anna to give to the other children. Whatever the form and degree of being seen as strange, children with autism suffer from and have to cope with shame, embarrassment, and humiliation. And parents have to cope with both their own embarrassment and the pain of seeing their child viewed as odd and not infrequently shunned, teased, or bullied by other children and adults as well. Children with autism often employ a protective wall of denial and an impenetrable displacement of attention to a systematizing activity with objects – only to appear odder to others. The narratives of Anna, Gus, and Owen describe how parents and child struggled with the problem of how each appeared to others so that all of these three talented children became accomplished, effective, enlivened adults.

Turning on to human relatedness

Anna, age five and a half, in a book store where she had previously been, in a sudden dramatic burst of interest and recognition turned on to human relatedness. The cartoon animals in a Disney comic book with their muted facial affects became anthropomorphic for Anna in their interactions and conversations. Anna's step-by-step preparation for this moment of recognition, absolutely necessary for it to happen, was long and arduous. Each step involved two phases. The first phase was to find a way to stimulate Anna's interest despite her strong inclination to turn off. This phase required building on an existing inclination or well formed intentional pattern of Anna's. Direct appeal for her to learn by rote teaching without activating an existing interest would fail to overcome her autistic disconnect from responsiveness to involvement with and pressure from others. The second phase was for Anna on her own to discern a sense of purpose for what Dr. T and others had introduced into her awareness. In her detailed account of the required preparation for turning on Dr. T describes six steps.

Step 1: Dr. T's decision to have three-year-old Anna with her at all times

Stimulus for Anna's interest: previously, caretakers were too random for Anna to build a system of clear expectation about those regarded as other. Now with Dr. T having her with her – waking, dressing, feeding, taking her along to Dr. T's work, and going to stores (the latter more easily apt to arouse Anna's interest), Anna could build a more consistent category of self with a specific other. Building and maintaining a category, distinguishing it from other categories, is a stimulus for interest for both autistic and well-adapted children.

Discerning a use, a sense of purpose: Anna could now recognize the purpose for her of interactional (not intersubjective) looking to her mother for the satisfaction of a wide variety of needs – feeding, clothing, toys, safety guidance, and especially places to go where she could get things she wanted. For Anna, Dr. T was the big other with whom she lived her life in parallel. Now she could experience the value of close approximation with a caretaking other – not yet mother and daughter or Mommy and Anna.

Step 2: Dr. Traugott's screaming Anna's name from behind her

Stimulus for Anna's interest: More than Anna having no interest in responding to her name or being talked to or with, she had an intense aversion to being pulled out from behind her autistic shield. By standing behind Anna, Dr. Taugott eliminated one source of resistance – response to the face. The screaming assault on Anna's ear drums created an aversive stimulus greater than Anna's aversion to responding – Anna now had an interest in stopping the auditory assault. Turning her head now had a purpose – she could stop the screaming.

Discerning a use, a sense of purpose: As noted Anna's first purpose was to counter the distress. Dr. Taugott did not leave her new pattern-building there. She added a positive use for Anna to respond – a banana candy – and gradually the purpose of Anna's turning her head when her name was spoken shifted from removing an aversive stimulus to getting a desired treat.

Step 3: Mrs. Golovina's use of a whole body gestural shift in posture to get Anna to sit and observe

Stimulus for Anna's interest: Mrs. Golovina demonstrated to Dr. T that by a forceful whole body gestural signal Anna could be influenced to respond to verbal instructions. Humans have a built-in response to movements observed in their peripheral vision. For example, when standing on a bus and talking to a friend, if a person needing you to move out of her way approaches, you shift your body as needed without reflection. With a child with autism, a balance exists between the turn off to human emotion-based verbal influence and the stir of interest to respond to a gestural cue for body placement. Mrs. G demonstrated how Dr. T could use her physical size to create a gesture powerful enough to stimulate Anna's interest in moving in accordance with her guidance.

Discerning a use, a sense of purpose: The movement itself did not convey a purpose. The purpose entered the picture when the movement permitted Anna to do something – see an interesting scene, play with an object, find a toy, solve a math problem.

Step 4: Dr. T's presentation of the elephant and bird cards in order to build Anna's vocabulary

Stimulus for Anna's interest: Dr. T combined the physical gestural guidance of Mrs. G with her own creative compounding of multiple levels of stimulation. The card presentation itself required presenting and removing cards at a pace fast enough to keep Anna's short attention span from triggering her retreat to an autistic state. (Anna's attention span when in pursuit of her solitary interests was fine.) Dr. T's solution for activating and maintaining her daughter's interest was to provide multiple sensory stimuli – words, colors, shapes, physical objects, and, because Anna was so very musically responsive, the piano.

Discerning a use, a sense of purpose: For Dr. T the purpose of exposing Anna to the cards was for her to activate enough interest for Anna to learn words and build a vocabulary: the cross-model stimuli worked around Anna's resistance to rote learning that for Anna would be without purpose. For Anna, the purpose was to solve a puzzle of what connects to what. In this way, Anna could form a new system through categorizing and differentiating words that connected with images, colors, sounds and touch.

Step 5: Exposing Anna to another symbolic system – math

Stimulus for Anna's interest: building on Anna's success in learning vocabulary, Dr. T decided to expose Anna to a system for which she felt her daughter was well prepared to respond to with interest – the systemizing of numbers. Discerning a use, a sense of purpose: Anna's sense of purpose was originally the pleasure of arranging numbers as though they were simply more abstract objects like concrete pieces of Lego. To make the use of math expand to mastery of Anna's engagements with the pragmatic world, Dr. T opened a bank account for her daughter and had her inform the bank teller the different amounts of money she needed for purchases.

Step 6: Taking Anna to the book store where she discovered a powerful use for her vocabulary

Stimulus for Anna's interest: pictures of animate objects interacting with each other were without the turn off of the pressure of human faces full of emotion that Anna couldn't decode. Now she could use words to decode the interactions occurring in the pictures. What the Disney characters did and said was more than interesting – it stimulated a total absorption.

Discerning a use, a sense of purpose: Anna had the sudden realization of a monumentally powerful use – the pictures and the words told a story of what people do and feel about each other.

The turn on of adapting infants

In contrast to the series of steps needed for Anna to "turn on," typical development occurs more as a continuous turning on to and shifting between human relatedness, skill in dealing with the environment, and physiological regulation. The lived experience of typical development in infancy involves an emergent unfolding of distinct but integrally interrelated interests and purposes, affects, intentions, and goals. This integrated unfolding begins in infancy.

Mother approaches. Mother and baby make eye contact. Baby leans forward. Mother prepares her breast, chucks baby's face. Baby fixes on the nipple and begins to suck. Mother says, "Oh you were really hungry" and chatters comments throughout their interaction. Baby releases the nipple and looks up as mother looks down and says "Hi, hi there little one." Baby begins to fuss. Mother says, "You have a bubble" and puts baby up to her shoulder. Baby stops fussing as her eyes fix on objects in her surround. Mother taps on her back, gas bubble is released and feeding is resumed.

The continuity and flow of the well adapted infant's turn on to human relatedness as central to multiple shifting motivations and feelings differs greatly from Anna's need for a step-by-step progress – responding to her name, gaining a vocabulary of words as designators along with their musicality, being systematically exposed to stores, restaurants, the library, etc. – leading and facilitating a dramatic moment of turning on to an elementary understanding of human intentions and feelings. The moments of mother–neonate eye contact, of subtle moving toward, of mimicking as with tongue extrusion, of alerting to the musicality of higher pitch speech, all seem so natural, so mundane, that the little miracle of the responsive pair turning on to each other is easily overlooked. Research findings definitively contradict the long-held view of early life as a period of oceanic isolation, an undifferentiated state, and blooming, buzzing, confusion (James, 1890). Infants at three months clearly discriminate between mini-dramas of a figure being helped or hindered to fulfill an intention and achieve a goal (Hamlin, Wynn, & Blum, 2010; Lichtenberg, Lachmann, & Fosshage, 2016). The infant eye averts from the hinderer and looks at the helper (at five months the infant reaches for the helper). At four months the pattern of infant–mother relatedness is so well formed that observations of face-to-face coordination serve as a reliable predictor of the one-year-old's mode of secure or insecure attachment (Beebe et al, 2010). Unlike the sudden turning on of Anna, the well adapted infant's turning on to his/her mother (and others) is a subtle nuanced development of interlocking capacities – each reinforcing and enhancing the functioning of the other: recognition of repeated experiences with each individual (and pet); sensing the affect and intentions of another and the interplay with one's own; picking up the rhythms and inter-play of conversation – the pauses, turn-taking, and the musicality of affective expression; assessing the meaning of the movements and gestures of caregiv-ers; responding to affirmation, a sense of commonality, safety, and inclusion; and forming an important emergent life-long basic hedonic tone of being loved and loveable. These interlocking capacities of the infant doer doing are the essential framework that provides the scaffolding onto which language, mentalizing, and social mores are added in increasing complexity.

The contrast between the lived experience of children with autism and well adapted children takes many forms that derive from the presence or absence of an integrated synthetic sense of relatedness. The interest and pur-pose that Dr. T helped Anna to build step-by-step is seamlessly formed and internalized in the healthy development of a sense of self as a doer doing, initiating and taking in, activating and responding. Transitions between the affects, intentions and goals of the attachment, affiliative, caregiving, exploratory, sensual, aversive, and physiological systems are relatively smooth in healthy development but often difficult, sometimes very dif-ficult, to make for the child with autism. Once in a solitary exploratory/systematizing activity the autistic child strongly resists the call from others to transition to another motivated activity and goal. Integrative goals and smooth transitioning is facilitated by the mutual self with other regulation that emerges from secure attachment and by the sense of having a benign other calling for a response in an ambiance of goodwill. It took Anna and Dr. T many arduous steps to achieve that kind of self with other regulation.

Each of the myriad interactions of caregivers and infants facilitates the emergence of one or another of the interlocking capacities and the buildup of mutual self and other regulation. The combined result is that the well adapted infant is deeply interested (turned on) to his exchanges with car-egivers initially and, in expanding contexts, with others. Anna had not been at all interested in recognizing, knowing, or responding to anyone until she turned on to Donald Duck and his friends, and then she wanted more and more!

When infants with a full potential for taking the pathway to intimacy are responded to lovingly by caregivers, the infants develop a positive core sense of self. Their experience of identity reflects an intersubjective ambiance of pleasurable sensuality. They take pride in being a responsive doer doing with caring sensitive others. In contrast, the limitations in human responsiveness, sensitivities, and social ineptness of children with autism lead them and their family to feel puzzled, discouraged, shamed, and humiliated. This personal feeling state and the surrounding negative ambiance causes a child similar to Anna to turn off and stay turned off to interactions with others. Having this turned off wall of resistance to face-to-face and other intimate engagements, children with autism can easily be incorrectly regarded as having no core sense of self. And so it seemed to many about Anna until her turning on. But Anna (and her mother) had an appreciation of her success on the pathway to mastery of her inanimate environment as a systematizer and builder. It is significant that Anna, like a well adapted child her age (but probably with greater intensity and focus), was turned on to solving math problems, constructing Lego buildings, and cataloguing trams, all challenges that allowed her to exercise her strong proclivity for solitary systematizing. And Anna's later pride and confidence were dramatically revealed in her twice refusing to be held back in schools for social lapses when she knew she learned her course work as well as any of her classmates. Turned on and in school relating to other children, Anna fixed their names for herself when they were out of the room by rearranging the chairs and putting a card with each classmate's name on their respective chair. Anna like her mother had (and has) a core sense of determination enhanced by creativity.

Early steps that unfold and integrate in adaptive development

For Anna's treatment, for her to turn on, required many steps in sequence each necessary for the next to be possible. For neonates and infants fully prepared for adaptive development, many steps are also necessary. The crucial difference is that these steps begin at birth (some in utero), form, fold into one another, and coalesce and integrate holistically moment-to-moment, day-to-day, and month-to-month in the first year and beyond.

Step 1 – Attachment: Neonates are prepared by evolution to respond to faces and sound frequencies within the range of the human voice. From their experience in utero, neonates are prepared to respond differentially to their biological mother's whole being from the sound of her voice heard externally and vibrating internally, her smell, and rhythms. The focus of their gaze is more accurate for objects about eight inches away – the exact distance from the mother's eyes when the infant is held in the normal breast or bottle-feeding position (Stern, 1977). Neonates will look for longer periods of time at line drawings of a human face than dots. By two weeks they will look at their mother's face longer than at a stranger's and will also look at the mother's face longer if she is talking to them (Carpenter, 1974). Neonates respond to the mother's chattering at them in a way that suggests participation in a dialogue. By eight weeks infants respond to the mother's chattering with definable pre-speech activities. It is important to recognize that infants experience their mothers not as bits and pieces of stimuli   a sound plus a sight that they have to put together laboriously – but as an integrated whole. The nature of this integrated whole is interactional, that is, mother the speaker (her articulating face, her vocalizations, her movements, and her affect) form a category – a narrative, that is coordinated with the infant's responses, vocalizations, affect, movements, and mimicry (Lichtenberg, 1989). The same innate responsiveness that creates this early attachment (bonding) experience with the biological mother enables infants to form a similar differential response to any persistent maternal caregiver (maternal in function not necessarily in gender). The affective quality that solidifies the path to attachment is being and feeling safe in the hands of a caring other. This affect "I am safe with her" plus the affects stirred by mirroring affirmations becomes integrated as a nonverbal imagistic story of her and my face, her and my sounds, her and my touch, and by three months her and my smile.

Step 2 – Communication: From the first cry to the calming of the distress in a feeding to the folding into the receptive arms of a caregiver, neonates and mothers convey information that each needs to be optimally responsive to the other. Caregivers' success in picking up and responding to the nonverbal narratives of the infant's needs and intentions facilitates the formation and functioning of the attachment, sensual, aversive, and exploratory motivational systems. Verbal communication – major steps for Anna and all humans is not necessary to form and tell a story to oneself and others. Dogs are wonderful communicators of their stories "I love you," "take me out," "I'm angry or hurt," "I do (or don't) want to be with you." All this is told by body movement, bark, head gesture, eye movement and focus. And dogs understand the meanings of human verbal communication about both emotions and intentions. So dogs and infants do not need words to form and tell stories of I like, I don't like, I want, I don't want, I look toward, I look away. And infants can and do form images that tell meaningful stories to themselves and others – as do humans all their lives in dreams, mind wandering, reveries, fantasies, and visual arts. But without words, human life, as with people with mutism, is barren in relatedness and communication both to others and to oneself. Humans evolved language and especially conversational language to bind people in groups enabling the enjoyment of commonality and kinship. Motherese begins at birth in the caregivers engaging musicality in her chatter to the baby.

Each language has its own basic elements of speech, pronunciation, and musicality: its vowels, glides, timbre, and pitch contours; its pre-voice and delayed voice onset time; its timing cued to turn taking and opening to response. Even before birth – "Infants read to from Dr. Seuss books while in utero evidence recognition of the sound pattern after birth" (DeCasper & Fifer, 1980). Recognition only occurs with the Seuss books they have been read to. This means that by birth, infants can process phonological contrasts. Normal infants are innately responsive to any language or languages they hear daily. This responsiveness applies to any language humans have created anywhere in the world. The universal responsiveness to any known language does not last. At 12 months and after infants can no longer automatically pick up any of the languages they had not been exposed to. This suggests that infants in the second half of the first year are restrictively sensitive to the nuances of languages spoken to and around them by people from whom they are seeking safety, mirroring, and twinship commonality.

When exposed to synthetic sounds that are not found in any human language, six-month-old infants who could detect vowel changes readily in the language they are exposed to responded differently. "They could neither differentiate automatically nor be trained to in spite of rewarding" (Lichtenberg, 1989, p. 74; Eimas et al., 1971). Thus, picking up and responding to speech and the non-verbal early stories it tells is innate. What then is different for a child like Anna? While communication (step 2) can be studied academically as a development sequence of nonverbal and then verbal skills in infancy, step 2 and step 1 are not independent. The two steps – attachment and communication – are intimately entwined and dependent on each other. Without face-to-face coordination, sharing of affects, chatter and vocalizing, and all the other interactions of infancy, words have no meaning. Meaning comes from the arousal of interest by the impact of recognizing and sharing affects, intentions, and purpose. A feeding, a shared look, a burping, a look around the room all involve an affect, an intention, and a purpose. Communication in the form of maternal commentary and infant vocalization provides an undramatic but indispensable accompaniment to what the two doers are doing. with each other. Not until relatively recently has the significance of early attachment and communication been recognized as precursors necessary for the older infant to become verbal. With autistic infants like Anna, when steps 1 and 2 are badly compromised; we recognize how its absence adversely affects the to-be-mute at age five otherwise smart little girl.

Step 3 – Regulation and power: Each child emerges from infancy with a sense of being able to self-regulate in respect to particular affects, intentions, and goals while needing help from caregivers in other motivational areas. And each child will have an implicit recognition of whether the benefit of his regulation accrues to him, to the caregiver regulator, or to both. The more he senses implicitly that it benefits him or both the more he can feel pride in his power to control his impulses and to please others. This is power in a positive sense in comparison to the power of opposition – of thwarting the unwelcome imposition from others. Thus, the no in gesture and the no in words at the end of the first year – the no so necessary for regulation – may convey to the self (and to others) a sense of power: when I self-regulate and I don't hit or bite, grab or drop, gobble down, or mess up – I can feel pride in my power and in my being judged to be a good boy as reflected in Mother and Father's face. Alternatively, when I become oppositional and antagonistic or turn away and withdraw (not usually as massive as for Anna) – I feel a sense of power to negate and obstruct and an identity as uncontrolled and uncontrollable, obstinate and rebellious, and a sense of shame along with the power.

The yes and no of regulation in infancy takes on a number of forms that distinguish the types of attachment. Secure attachment involves positive self and self with other regulation. Ambivalent attachment involves a regulation in which the infant is preoccupied with whether she is being accepted or rejected. Based on the mother–child interplay is she being drawn to or aversive to? Avoidant attachment involves the infant's aversive oppositional regulatory stance (a core pattern exaggerated for the autistic child). And the one-year-old who evidences a disorganized attachment demonstrates a severe problem in regulation (exaggerated in the wildness of the autistic child).

During infancy, body physiological regulation is a central focus for caregiver and child. Physiological regulation is based on the ability of both mother and infant to pick up and coordinate signals. For an infant, sensations tell him he is hungry or full, needs to urinate, and/or defecate, breathe more easily, drift to sleep, relieve stomach gas, have a bumped or scratched knee soothed. The caregiver needs to recognize and respond to the externally communicative signal of the need or distress. This leads to an integrated sequence of signals – sensation, external indicator, recognition (which cry means what?), and response. As the child's negative sensations abate as the result of the caregiver's recognition and ministrations, the infant builds an implicit sense of my mother gets me and we make an effective pair. The successful integration of physiological patterns and relational themes constitutes effective regulation that is first infant–caregiver–infant and with further development increasingly the child's own. Much emotion is generated in the doing of the regulating: for the baby, relief and appreciative love, for the mother, a struggle to recognize and puzzle out what and how she is being called on to activate or respond to, and how is her devotion to caregiving to balance with other activities without resentment. Positive and negative emotions stirred in the early interactions remain throughout life whenever there is a call for physiological self-regulation.

Parents provide mobiles, rattles, toys, and stuffed animals to capture their infants' interest. Nature offers changing light and shadow, sounds like rain and thunder. Pets move about and lick. For the infant the interest stirred by these attractors contributes to the enlivening of the sense of self and a challenge to the mother–child interaction. Does the caregiver recognize and support and/or sensitively modify the child's spontaneous flow of interest and the intentions that go with it? Recognition alone conveys a form of sharing. Recognition and facilitating or modifying adds a coloration to sharing – the sense of the caregiver as a helper. Non-recognition when the child needs assistance to support her interest or ignoring the child's intentions and overriding it with the parents own triggers a sense of the other as hinderer. Three-month-old infants make a definitive distinction between a helper and a hinderer and the emotion stirred by each. For a child to learn to play and to develop the skills needed to master the challenges of her environment, significant principles of regulation are required: don't run out into the street, glass will shatter, walls are not to draw on, shoe laces must be tied, toys must be shared when friends come over. When the infant's emergent interests and intentions to explore are recognized, guided, and helped, and a positive affect aroused, the skills and regulation will be comfortably internalized. When an infant's emergent interests and intentions are repeatedly ignored and abandoned or opposed and overridden, efforts to regulate will be responded to with rejection, obstinacy, and rebelled against.

The regulations of the sensual-sexual motivational system is focused mainly on the older child's seeking for sexual arousal. During infancy finger sucking, body rubbing and genital touch may be restricted based on cultural mores. Shaming is the parent's main weapon against culturally sanctioned self-arousal – less so if an activity like finger sucking is viewed as helpful self-soothing. While shaming may be used to prohibit any behavior viewed as bad, shame/humiliation (along with guilt and fear of retaliation from a parental rival – castration anxiety) is the central barrier for the regulation of sexual desire (Lichtenberg, 2008).

Step 4 – Hedonic tone: It has long been known that infants are affected by the feeling state of those around them. Maternal post-partum depression results in the child and adult being vulnerable to some form of dysphoria. Infants are not usually confronted by such an enveloping affect state although the sadness of a house in mourning, or the fear state of warfare or other traumas like being the child of a holocaust survivor – has predispositional effect. In contrast to these inescapable generalizing influences on hedonic tone, in ordinary experience the affects associated with the intentions and goals of each motivational system and the narratives that give meaning to them are relatively specific to the intentions and goals of the system: attachment and affiliation – safety, affirmation, commonality, affection, admiration, joy; physiologic regulation – sensations of discomfort and relief; exploration and assertion of preferences – interest, efficacy, and confidence; caregiving – altruism, and concern; aversive – fear, panic,

sadness, shame, humiliation, disdain; sensual-sexual-pleasurable sensations, and/or erotic arousal and excitement.

Regarding affective experience as either an enveloping predisposi-
tion or a series of many emotions specifically associated with particular
intentions and goals gives a limiting polarized view of hedonic tone. I
suggest that, in ordinary healthy adaptive development, the sense of self
as it emerges from infancy has an underlying abiding hum of an affective
tonality and that sensual (not sexual) experience is largely responsible
for its quality. The sensuality to which I am referring includes the up-
beat experience of face-to-face greeting, smiles, playful hide and seek,
mimicking, the musicality of an upper pitched maternal voice, the ten-
der caress of being held, the arousal in tickle and tease play, and the
thrill of being held up high by Daddy or riding on his shoulders. And
sensuality includes the pleasurable experience of calming and soothing,
drifting off to sleep with lullaby and Good Night Moon, of being rocked
and gently petted. An infant's use of a blanket as a transitional object
(Winnicott, 1960) illustrates the role of sensuality in creating a hedonic
tone. A blanket is selected for its sensual properties – its texture and
warmth, absorbing of smells, and ability to be molded against any part
of the body. The blanket's otherness lends itself to being a representative of or replacement for the comforting other – but a comforting other
under the command of the self. A blanket's otherness also facilitates its
being imagined as a reliably available playmate and friend. Along with
its otherness, the blanket also represents an extension of the self when it
is carried about or cried into. The balance between qualities of discrete
emotions and the generalized feeling states that emerge from an infant's
experiences with her blanket tilts heavily toward a hedonic tone.

The repetition of positive experiences as recurring daily states builds
expectancies and confidence. Non-verbal stories depict the experience of
being of being a doer doing both interacting with caregivers and when alone
watching a mobile, shaking a rattle, playing with toys, and self-soothing
with a blanket. I suggest the confidence that these positive expectations
will come to fruition is the source of an underlying attitude of optimism
and the hedonic tone that accompanies it. The optimistic attitude includes
the implicit belief that being loved and loving will be present or, if lost,
will be restored. The hedonic tone I have described derives directly from
the infant's attachment experience with his caretakers. But the infant's

lived experience includes awareness of the shifting emotions and atmospheric affects in his surround that don't directly involve him. That humans are born sensitive to affects in their surround is supported by the finding of contagion in the nursery when otherwise comfortable neonates will cry if they hear another cry. Do the parents work together well and lovingly? Do they have the ability to overcome obstacles? Is their relationship one of domination/submission with all the resentment that accompanies it? Are the parents generally disorganized, unable to plan and function together? Do they subject each other to the corrosive effect of contempt and disdain? I believe that infants and children who experience a positive intersubjective ambiance in their surround develop a deep implicit sense that in intersubjective exchanges good will generally prevails, or if lost will be restored.

For the older child and adult an expectation that differences and controversies will generally be responded to with goodwill becomes a conscious guiding organizing principle that has a positive effect in bringing about confirmation. I am suggesting that the hedonic tones, beliefs, and expectations begin as loosely formulated holistic sensibilities. These sensibilities underlie the later affectively rich narratives that give expression to differing motivational states. But whether positive or negative, hedonic tones are not inert sources of influence – they are active in their contribution to the ambiance that will emerge from every significant interpersonal relationship. Just as humans are very susceptible to an ambiance that has an effect on their personal development and on the environmental surround, they are constant creators of an ambiance that develops between them and any significant others.

The concurrently occurring steps – attachment, communication, regulation, and hedonic tone – begin as an enactment in which the mother's internal preparedness interacts with the temperament and evolutional preparedness of the neonate. This mother–infant interchange creates the specific recognition and connection between this particular baby and this particular mother. They turn to each other emotionally and physically. They communicate telling each other stories – "You're my sweet little baby" – "Mother comes smiles – nice"; "You are hungry" – "I greet your nipple with my sucking mouth." As they signal each other about their individual needs, feelings, intentions, purpose, and goals, they adjust their bodies and the pace and patterns of their mutual doings. With each doing – attachment, physiological regulation, interest, exploration, opposition or acceptance, caressing or soothing – a feeling of the moment emerges and along with it a broader emotional sensibility – an ambiance that belongs to the dyad and remains fundamental to the infant, child, and adults' affective dispositional state.

In comparison to the holistic experience of turn of ordinary infants, for Anna to turn on to human relatedness required a linear series of steps over a discrete period of time – each step necessary for the next to be effective. Each step was made possible by some quality or capacity that had developed largely outside of secure attachment. While for Anna and her mother sensual pleasure as an intersubjective experience was absent, Anna did have discrete areas of sensuality. Anna loved the feel of fabric that was soft and smooth, made her own choice of clothes, and enjoyed the feel and touch of dressing herself. She loved the color blue and wanted blue things in many forms. She enjoyed the sound of her mother's playing the violin but not the sound of the piano. She loved her bottle and later selected foods. After an initial reluctance and fear, she loved being in water and swimming. These sensual pleasures formed the background for Anna's post-turned-on enjoyment of dancing, traveling extensively to view nature, and finally intimacy with peers and a romance with a boyfriend.

To summarize: for ordinary adaptive development the turn on to human relatedness requires a series of interlocking steps all occurring in the same time period – each step enhancing the richness and efficacy of the other. As mother and infant offer their psychic readiness to join to create a safe haven for nurture and affection, each needs to tell the other what's up and find out what the other is conveying. In words and actions mothers tell their baby how he needs to be for her intention of the moment to succeed. And the baby in his facial and body messages tells his mother how she needs to be for him to be happy and relieved of distress. So in one holistic "package" infants and mothers learn to communicate with each other and regulate each other. And along with their interpersonal communication the infant learns to communicate with herself, and along with the mutual recognition, the infant learns to regulate herself.

Building a deeply felt connection through attachment, learning to communicate emotions, needs, intentions and goals, and engaging in mutual and self-regulation involves two distinct processes. One process responds to lived experience by forming differing categories of familiar repeated psychic events. These categories self-organize and self-stabilize into motivational systems that exist in dialectic tension with other motivational systems opening the way to shifts, enhancements, and reorganizations of intentions and goals. In contrast to the functional focus of this process leading to increasing adaptive differentiation, another process tends toward broadened integration and synthesis. In *Narrative and Meaning* (Lichtenberg, Lachmann, & Fosshage, 2017), we pointed to this process as it applied to broad "master" narratives, generalized cultural and religious myths, the broad total effect of a great piece of music, and the emergence of a generalized sense of personal, family, and cultural identity. These examples all apply to the narrative themes and sensibilities of the motivational systems of an older child and adult. Returning to the infant in the first year, the integration synthetic process involving the four steps, when adaptive, centers on the play our of affects associated with sensuality in each step – the loving exchange of looks, of the musical contours of speech, of mouth, skin, body, genital rubbings and rhythms, of body-sensations when held, rocked, bathed, naked and being diapered. Each of these positive feelings may originate in a particular sensory mode but easily spread across mode (Stern, 1985). Two generalizing lived experiences result. First, the feelings from the attachment connection, communication, and regulation each influence how the other is experienced. The turn on is not attachment and the communication, and the regulation – the turn on is to each as it folds into and influences the other holistically. Second, I believe a healthy adaptive core sense of self emerges from a sensually centered mode of experience leading to an optimistic belief in self and others, along with confidence that generally good will prevail in many if not most human relations. In addition, pleasurable experience and an underlying implicit hedonic tone will be activated by an aesthetic feel for the uplift from the beauty of the creations of nature and man. Even at is most consolidated, a positive hedonic tone is subject to negative influence by persistent stress or acute trauma. But even when turned off, this central sensibility is a powerful resource for a turn on by treatment.

References

Ankenman, K., Elgin, J., Sullivan, K., Vincent, L., & Bernier R. (2014). Nonverbal and verbal cognitive discrepancy profiles in autism spectrum disorders: influence of age and gender. *American Journal on Intellectual and Developmental Disabilities*, 119(1): 84–99.

Beebe, B., Jaffe, J., Markese, S., Buck, K., Chen, H., Cohen, P., Bahrick, L., Andrews, H., & Feldstein, S. (2010). The origins of 12-month attachment: a microanalysis of 4-month mother–infant interaction. *Attachment & Human Development*, 12: 3–141.

Beebe, B., & Lachmann, F. M. (2002). *Infant research and adult treatment: co-constructing interactions*. Hillsdale, NJ: The Analytic Press.

Bernstein, Robert J., & Cantor-Cooke, Robin (2017). *Uniquely normal: tapping the reservoir of normalcy to treat autism*. Arlington, TX: Future Horizons, Inc.

Brandchaft, B., Doctors, S., & Sorter, D. (2010). *Toward an emancipator psychoanalyses*. New York: Routledge.

Carpenter, G. (1974). Mother's face and the newborn. *New Scientist*, 61: 742.

Courchesne, V., Meilleur, A. A., Poulin-Lord, M. P., Dawson, M., & Soulières, I. (2015). Autistic children at risk of being underestimated: school-based pilot study of a strength-informed assessment. *Molecular Autism*, Mar 6; 6: 12.

DeCasper, A. J., & Fifer, W. P. (1980). Of human bonding: newborns prefer their mother's voices. *Science*, 208: 1174–1176.

Eimas, P., Siqueland, W., Judezyk, P., & Vigerito, J. (1971). Speech perception in infants. *Science*, 218: 138–380.

Ellenby, W. (2018). *Autism uncensored: pulling back the curtain*. Virginia Beach, VA: Koehler Books.

Fivaz-Depeursinge, E., & Corboz-Warnery, A. (1999). *The primary triangle*. New York: Basic Books.

French, L., & Kennedy, E. M. M. (2018). Annual research review: early intervention for infants and young children with, or at-risk of, autism spectrum disorder: a systematic review. *Journal of Child Psychology and Psychiatry*, Apr; 59(4): 444–456.

Frith, U. (1992). *Autism and Asperger syndrome*. Cambridge: Cambridge University Press.

Hamlin, J. K., Wynn, K., & Bloom, P. (2010). Three-month olds show a negativity bias in their social interactions. *Developmental Science*, 13(6): 923–929.

James, W. (1890). *Principles of psychology*. New York: Holt.

Johnson, M. H. (2017). Autism as an adaptive common variant pathway for human brain development. *Developmental Cognitive Neuroscience*, 25: 5–11.

Kanner, L. (1943). Autistic disturbances of affective contact. *Nervous Child: Journal of Psychopathology, Psychotherapy, Mental Hygiene, and Guidance of the Child*, 2: 217–250.

Kanner, L. (1949). Problems of nosology and psychodynamics of early infantile autism. *American Journal of Orthopsychiatry*, 19: 416–426.

Klin, A., Jones, W., Schultz, R., Volkmar, F., & Cohen, D. (2002). Defining and quantifying the social phenotype in autism. *American Journal of Psychiatry*, 159: 895–907.

Klin, A., Jones, W., Schulz, R., & Volkmar, F. (2003). The enactive mind, or from actions to cognition: lessons from autism. *Philosophical Transactions of the Royal Society B*, 358: 345–380.

Kohut, H. (1984). *How does analysis cure?* Chicago, IL: University of Chicago Press.

Krueger, K. K. (2013). *Minimally verbal school-aged children with autism: communication, academic engagement and classroom quality. UCLA*. ProQuest ID: Krueger_ucla_0031D_11894. Merritt ID: ark:/13030/m59p4fkk. Retrieved from https://escholarship.org/uc/item/1329g9pk.

Lichtenberg, J. D. (1989). *Psychoanalysis and motivation*. Hillsdale, NJ: Analytic Press.

Lichtenberg, J. D. (2008). *Sensuality and sexuality across the divide of shame*. New York: The Analytic Press.

Lichtenberg, J., Lachmann, F., & Fosshage, J. (2011). *Psychoanalysis and motivational systems: a new look*. New York: Routledge.

Lichtenberg, J., Lachmann, F. & Fosshage, J. (2016). *Enlivening the self: the first year, clinical enrichment, and the wandering mind*. New York: Routledge.

Lichtenberg, J., Lachmann, F., & Fosshage, J. (2017). *Narrative and meaning*. New York: Routledge.

Lovaas, I. (1977). *The autistic child: language development through behavior modification*. New York: Irvington Publishers.

Magán-Maganto, M., Jónsdóttir, S. L., Sánchez-García, A. B., García-Primo, P., Hellendoorn, A., Charman, T., Roevers, H., Dereu, M., Moilanen, I., Muratori, F., Posada de la Paz, M., Rogé, B., Oosterling, I. J., Yliherva, A., & Canal-Bedia, R. (2017). Measurement issues: building a theoretical framework for autism spectrum disorders screening instruments in Europe. *Child and Adolescent Mental Health*.

Mottron, L. (2017). Should we change targets and methods of early intervention in autism, in favor of a strengths-based education? *European Child and Adolescent Psychiatry*, 26(7): 815–825.

National Institutes of Health (2010). Workshop on nonverbal school-aged children with autism. Bethesda, Maryland, 13–14 April 2010. https://www.nidcd.nih.gov/research/workshops/nonverbal-school-aged-children-autism/2010/summary. Retrieved September 26, 2018.

Newman, J. (2017). *To Siri with love: a mother, her autistic son, and the kindness of machines*. New York: Harper Collins.

Pickett, A., Pullara, O., O'Grady, J., & Gordon, B. (2009). Speech acquisition in older nonverbal individuals with autism: a review of features, methods and prognosis. *Cognitive Behavioral Neurology*, 22(1): 1–21.

Piven, J., Elison, J., & Zylka, M. (2017). Toward a conceptual framework for early brain and behavior development in autism. *Molecular Psychiatry*, 00: 1–10.

Sacks, O. (1995). *An anthropologist on Mars*. New York: Alfred A. Knopf.

Sanders, L. (1983). To begin with: reflections on ontogeny. In J. Lichtenberg & S. Kaplan (Eds.) *Reflections on self-psychology* (pp. 85–104). Hillsdale, NJ: The Analytic Press.

Schultz, R. PhD, Gauthier, I. PhD, Klin, A. PhD, Fulbright, R. MD, Anderson, A. PhD, Volkmar, F. MD, Skudlarski, P. PhD, Lacadie, C. BS, Cohen, D. MD, & Gore, J. PhD. (2000). Abnormal ventral temporal cortical activity during face discrimination among individuals with autism and Asperger syndrome. *Archives of General Psychiatry*, 57: 331–340.

Stern, D. N. (1977). *The first relationship*. Cambridge, MA: Harvard University Press.

Stern, D. N. (1985). *The interpersonal world of the infant*. New York: Basic Books.

Suskind, R. (2014). *Life animated: a story of sidekicks, heroes, and autism*. Los Angeles, CA: Kingswell.

Tager-Flusberg, H., & Kasari, C. (2013). Minimally verbal school-aged children with autism spectrum disorder: the neglected end of the spectrum. *Autism Research*, Dec; 6(6): 468–478.

Tronick, E. (2002). A model of infant mood states and Sanderian affective waves. *Psychoanalytic Dialogues*, 12: 73–99.

Tronick, E., & Cohn, J. (1989). Infant–mother face-to-face interaction: age and gender differences in coordination and the occurrence of miscoordination. *Child Development*, 60: 85–92.

WHO. (2013). Meeting report: autism spectrum disorders & other developmental disorders: from raising awareness to building capacity. Geneva Switzerland: World Health Organization, 16–18 September 2013.

Winnicott, D. W. (1960). The theory of the parent–infant relationship. *International Journal of Psychoanalysis*, 41: 585–595.

Index